D1173468

TO

FROM

OCCASION

The James Code
© 2015 by O. S. Hawkins

Published in Nashville, Tennessee, by Thomas Nelson. Thomas Nelson is a registered trademark of HarperCollins Christian Publishing, Inc.

Cover design by Bruce DeRoos at Left Coast Design.
Interior design by Kristy L. Edwards.

Thomas Nelson titles may be purchased in bulk for educational, business, fund-raising, or sales promotional use. For information, please e-mail SpecialMarkets@ThomasNelson.com.

ISBN-13: 978-0-7180-4013-0
ISBN-13: 978-0-7180-9956-5 (custom)

Printed in the United States of America

15 16 17 18 19 RRD 6 5 4 3 2 1

www.thomasnelson.com

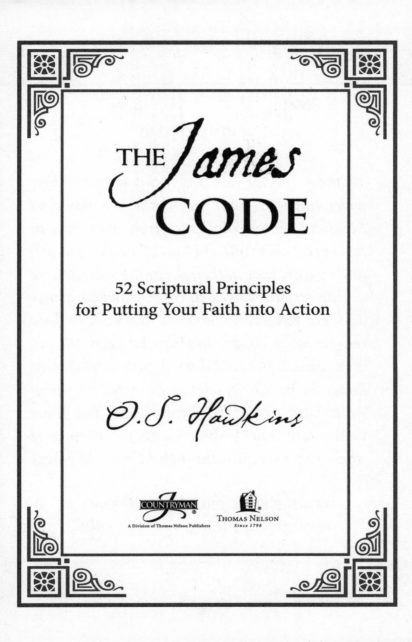

THE *James* CODE

52 Scriptural Principles for Putting Your Faith into Action

O. S. Hawkins

COUNTRYMAN®
A Division of Thomas Nelson Publishers

THOMAS NELSON
Since 1798

DEDICATION

To those special and sacrificial pastors, their wives, and in most cases, their widows in Mission:Dignity who have given their lives to serving others so often in "out of the way places," and who are now in their declining years. While in ministry they lived in church-owned homes and received smaller salaries, and now, in their retirement years, are in financial need. We are on a mission to bring them dignity, and it is an honor being Christ's hand extended to them. All royalties from The James Code, The Jesus Code, *and* The Joshua Code *go to support these sweet servants through Mission:Dignity.*

(Learn more about Mission:Dignity at www.guidestone.org/missiondignity.)

TABLE *of* CONTENTS

INTRODUCTION: MEET JAMES

*A*llow me to introduce you to James, the writer of the New Testament letter that bears his name.

I want to begin by telling you who he is *not*. The James I want you to meet is not the more well-known James of the Gospels—one of the Sons of Thunder, the brother of John the Beloved, and the fisherman son of Zebedee. That more well-known James often found himself in the inner circle, one of three men with whom Jesus often chose to be during His most significant and unforgettable moments, there on the Mount of Transfiguration and in Gethsemane's dark garden that fateful night. Shortly after the ascension of the resurrected Jesus, this James of the Gospels met a martyr's death by the sword of King Herod. He was the first apostle to die for his faith.

The James I want you to meet was not in our Lord's inner circle, but probably no one knew Jesus in a more up-close-and-personal way than this James did. The James whose words we will explore during the next few weeks was, in fact, Jesus' own half-brother, the natural-born son of Mary and Joseph. Literally, our James was Jesus' little brother. They undoubtedly spent years sharing the same room, playing together on the dusty streets of Nazareth, and working side by side in their father's carpentry shop.

During Jesus' earthly life, James apparently could not bring himself to believe that his Brother was the long-awaited Messiah. James didn't become a believer until after the resurrection. According to Paul, after Jesus rose from the grave, "he appeared to James, then to all the apostles" (1 Corinthians 15:7 NIV). Somewhere, privately and personally, before the risen Lord revealed Himself to any others, He met with James—and His little brother's life was never the same. After his encounter with his older Brother, with the victorious-over-death God-man, James grew in faith, became the undisputed leader of the Jerusalem Church, and convened the Jerusalem Council to determine whether Gentiles needed to follow the law of Moses and Jewish traditions in order to become followers of Jesus (Acts 15). The apostle Paul referred to James as a pillar of the church (Galatians 2:9). And tradition tells us that James was so devoted to prayer that he was given the nickname "Camel Knees" because of the calluses resulting from the hours he spent on his knees.

Today we are two thousand years removed from James's writing, yet his letter remains as relevant to us as the Internet's morning news. Why? Because in these 108 verses is a sort of code—a James Code—that outlines how we can put our faith into action in the normal traffic patterns of everyday life. If you're like me, your challenge is not knowing what Christ calls us to do, but actually doing it; the challenge is practicing with our lives what we know in our minds and proclaim with our lips. In every paragraph James reminds us that when we are walking in the Holy Spirit, we will not be wearing out the seats of our pants but the soles of our shoes. James challenged us to put shoe leather to what we say we believe. In his own words, we who name Jesus our Savior and Lord are to be "doers of the word, and not hearers only" (James 1:22). The importance of being doers was powerfully illustrated for me on the other side of the world.

AN OBJECT LESSON

For years, my wife, Susie, and I have made annual pilgrimages to Israel. Of the many sights and sounds of the Holy Land that I've grown to love, two in particular have captured my complete attention. In the north and teeming with aquatic life of many kinds, the vibrant Sea of Galilee is a beautiful blue and, in many places, as clear as crystal. The other body of water, in the south, is the Dead Sea, and it is called "dead" for good reason. There is no life in its stagnant water, and the putrid sulfur smell is nauseating.

What makes these two bodies of water so different? First, the Sea of Galilee has an inlet: the Jordan River flows from its source near Mount Hermon in the north into the Sea of Galilee. On its southern shore, the Sea of Galilee also has an outlet: water flows into the Jordan and on through the Great Rift Valley. Like the Sea of Galilee, the Dead Sea has an inlet: the Jordan flows into it. But the Dead Sea has no outlet: it takes in, but does not give out.

And this is the point of *The James Code*. Vibrant believers not only take in, but they also give out. They put the Word

they receive (input) into action (output). Yes, they become "doers of the word, and not hearers only."

James's signal contribution to believers then and now is his warning that we could become so heavenly minded that we would be no earthly good. He challenged us not merely to have our minds and hearts focused on the heavenly message of Scripture, but also to act on that message so that, by being God's light and salt, we are doing good on this earth. James's letter is arguably the most practical of all the New Testament writings. In fact, it could be summed up with the famous Nike slogan "Just do it"!

If you're struggling to put your faith into action, the message of James is for you. And this devotional is designed to move that message from your heart to your hands, to move you from merely hearing God's commands to actually doing them. And you'll discover that James isn't speaking to us about faith *and* works, but about a faith *that* works. And this is what our dying world needs to see!

Let's get started!

1 STRESS: FIVE FASCINATING FACTS

James, a bondservant of God and of the Lord Jesus Christ, to the twelve tribes which are scattered abroad: Greetings.

—JAMES 1:1

Stress! Perhaps no other word is used as much to describe the culprit, the scapegoat, the excuse of modern man. Many of the problems in our homes and with our health seem to relate to this stress factor. But stress has been around through the ages.

Note, for instance, that James addressed his epistle "to the twelve tribes which are scattered abroad," to those early Christians who had fled Jerusalem. The Greek word James used to describe this is *diaspora*, from which we get our words *dispersed* and *dispersion*. The word picture is of someone scattering seeds.

After the martyrdom of Stephen in Acts 7, the Christians in Jerusalem came under increasing persecution from the Roman Empire. They refused the Romans' demand to confess "Caesar is Lord." Instead, they insisted there was only one Lord, the Lord Jesus Christ. Thus, the Bible informs us, "They were all scattered . . . except the apostles" (Acts 8:1).

James was writing to those believers who had to leave their

homes, their jobs, their properties—everything. Talk about stress! Yet God permitted these early believers to experience the scattering and the resulting stress for a purpose. Had these believers stayed in Jerusalem, chances are the gospel would not have spread so completely through the known world. Everywhere these early followers of Jesus were scattered, they shared the good news of Christ's redemptive work, and in just one generation the gospel spread throughout the Roman Empire.

James was writing to people facing "various trials" (James 1:2). He was instructing them—and now instructs us—on how to deal with stress and pressures that come our way. James addressed stress long before the multitudinous volumes of books on modern stress were written. He was writing to people who were experiencing stress and about to crack under pressure. He was writing to those of us who are trying to live out what we say we believe. Consequently, James was extremely practical as he encouraged his readers to live out a faith that works.

As I type these words, I think about those who initially read James's letter almost two thousand years ago. Some of them were wives and mothers at their wits' end. Uprooted from their homes and miles away from what they had always known, they were now trying hard to keep their families together. James was also writing to children trying to deal with new surroundings and uncertain futures, suddenly living in a completely different culture. Also hearing these words were men who had lost their jobs, their land, everything they had spent a lifetime building. These men and women undoubtedly felt as though they were hanging by a thread. They were living under tremendous pressure and great stress.

In our modern world, the moment we hear the word *stress*, we tense up, clench our fists, and grind our teeth—as if stress were our foe. Yet stress can be our friend. In fact, Dr. Kenneth Cooper has written a book titled *Can Stress Heal?* The subtitle gets to the heart of the issue: *Converting a major health hazard into a surprising health benefit.* Stress is often God's way of telling us that our life is out of balance. In fact, James was teaching that stress is a warning signal that can actually be one of life's greatest tools. Learning to effectively deal with high anxiety when it comes knocking at our door can result in longer, happier, and even healthier lives.

We might not know—as the Jews in James's day did—the stress of literally being uprooted from all we have known, nor the stress of crossing oceans in rickety wooden boats to find religious freedom, but those people who lived just a few years before we were born did not know the stresses of our modern world. Exponential change is happening all around us. We all face our own limits, whether they be limits to time, energy, health, or finances, and many of us are perilously close to burnout. Yet, as we keep hoping that the pace of life will eventually level out or slow down, it seems to keep getting faster and more intense.

That's why a great life skill is the ability to cope with stress and pressure. As we look closely at the words of James in the pages that follow, we'll see that he was addressing not just the stress and pressure of a first-century world but of our own fast-paced twenty-first-century experience as well. James's letter is not so much a theological exposé, like Romans. It's much more practical, focused on how to live out our faith in a pressure-packed world.

In the initial paragraphs of his letter, James revealed five fascinating facts about stress. First, stress is *predictable*. Stress happens, and it's not going away. Second, stress is *problematic*. If we don't learn to deal with stress, it can be detrimental and even destructive to our health, our homes, our happiness, and our hopes. Third, stress is *paradoxical*. James said to "count it all joy when you fall into various trials" (James 1:2). Now, *that* is a paradoxical thought if ever there was one! Fourth, stress is *purposeful*. Some of us go through the furnace of stress and come out like refined gold, better suited and prepared for a life of purpose. Finally, stress can be *profitable*. God can use stress for our good and His glory.

Those early believers were not the only ones living in a diaspora. In a very real sense, believers today are scattered all around the world, living in exile from our heavenly, eternal home. Thus, behind the hand of James is the hand of God Himself, writing to you and me at a point of personal need.

JUST DO IT!

Stress is a fact of life. It's not going away, and we all must deal with it. As you study James, begin to see yourself as the lone recipient of this letter: it's from God, through James, and to you personally. Listen to his seasoned and sage advice and put it into practice. Start thinking of stress as a friend, and not just a foe. Stress is there for a purpose.

2   STRESS IS PREDICTABLE

James, a bondservant of God and of the Lord Jesus Christ, to the twelve tribes which are scattered abroad: Greetings. My brethren, count it all joy when you fall into various trials.

—JAMES 1:1–2

*W*hat?!? James was telling us to count it all joy when we "fall into various trials"? Most of us count it joy when we escape the trials of life, not when we fall into them! And notice that James was not saying to count it joy *if* we fall into trials. He said we are to count it joy *when* we fall into them. Experiencing stress is not an *if*; it's a *when*. Stress is predictable: it is inevitable, inescapable, unavoidable. We all experience it. We can't avoid it. Stress happens.

In fact, we can read the Bible from cover to cover, and nowhere will we find the promise that we're immune to stress or sickness, exempt from trials or tribulations. Some, however, teach falsely that if we're living the Spirit-filled life, we'll have only smooth sailing on the sea of God's will. But may I remind you that our Lord Himself warned, "In the world you will have tribulation; but be of good cheer, I have overcome the world" (John 16:33).

Yes, stress is predictable. We can't avoid stress, but it can actually be good for us. Stress can, for instance, be a motivating factor: it can motivate us to make changes in our life or our lifestyle. However, too much stress coupled with not knowing how to deal with it can be detrimental mentally, spiritually, and physically. Stress can contribute to depression, which is real and rampant in our fast-paced society. Among its spiritual implications, stress and life's pressures can lead us, like Elijah of old, to run away from God's plan for us and find our own juniper tree where we sit in defeat and self-pity (1 Kings 19). Physically, stress prompts our body to pump adrenaline into our bloodstream, preparing us to fight or flee. If we do neither, the adrenaline remains in our system until our bodies break it down and slowly absorb it. High stress levels in our bodies over long periods of time can cause high blood pressure, ulcers, heart disease, headaches, and other serious health issues.

Although stress is predictable and can indeed have ramifications, it does not have to be our foe. Stress can be a friend. Consider that God never calls upon us to work harder than He did in the creation event—and He took the seventh day off! Many of our physical challenges are the result of our own bad decisions, and the same is true about mental challenges. Isaiah put it like this: "You will keep him in perfect peace, whose mind is stayed on You, because he trusts in You" (Isaiah 26:3). In the New Testament, the apostle Paul had his own prescription for stress: "Be anxious for nothing, but in everything by prayer and supplication, with thanksgiving, let your requests be made known to God; and the peace of God, which surpasses all understanding, will guard your hearts and minds through Christ Jesus" (Philippians 4:6–7).

James continued his instruction. We should count it joy when we face what? Trials. There is a difference between a trial and a temptation. Trials come from God to strengthen the Christian's ability to stand; temptations come from the Devil to cause the Christian to stumble. None of us can avoid trials. They are predictable. No matter who we are or how long we have journeyed in the Christian faith, we will face stress. The sooner we realize this fact, the sooner we can learn to deal with it. The tragedy of today's tranquilizer mentality is that it simply prolongs the day when we finally learn to deal with stress.

It is also important to note that James said we should count it joy when we "fall into" trials of various kinds. Interestingly, the Greek word used here is also used to describe the man in Jesus' parable who "went down from Jerusalem to Jericho and fell among thieves" (Luke 10:30). Here was a guy minding his own business. He rounded a corner and—WHAM!—he was suddenly surrounded by unexpected trouble. There was no warning, no time to run away. He "fell into" this trial, and this same thing happens to us at one time or another. We are sailing through life, going around the bend, and—WHAM!—we, too, "fall into various trials." Things are going pretty well, and then we get the doctor's report or the pink slip at the office . . . or the roof springs an expensive leak . . . or additional income tax is due . . . or the health insurance premium skyrockets beyond our ability to pay, or death comes knocking unexpectedly on a loved one's door.

None of us is exempt from falling into various trials. The New Testament writers constantly reminded us that trials are a part of life, and in that sense they are predictable. Peter put it like this:

> In this you greatly rejoice, though now for a little while, if need be, you have been grieved by various trials, that the genuineness of your faith, being much more precious than gold that perishes, though it is tested by fire, may be found to praise, honor, and glory at the revelation of Jesus Christ. (1 Peter 1:6–7)

No one ever had more trials come his way than Paul. He said that he served "the Lord with all humility, with many tears and trials which happened to me by the plotting of the Jews" (Acts 20:19). And even our Lord knew stress. He wasn't exempt from falling into various trials. In the upper room the evening before the crucifixion, He said to His disciples, "You are those who have continued with Me in My trials" (Luke 22:28).

Jesus knew better than anyone that stressful trials come our way, yet He never appeared to be stressed out. We never find Him wringing His hands or anxiously pacing. Instead we see Jesus get away, alone with His heavenly Father, from time to time. If He needed those times of solace and solitude, how much more do we?

As followers of Christ, we will encounter two basic kinds of trials: trials of correction and trials of perfection. God allows

them both. When we are out of His will for our lives, trials of correction often come our way. Just ask Jonah. He got into a major storm of correction and learned his lesson, corrected his way, and was greatly used by God. On the other hand, trials of perfection come to us when are in the will of God, when we are exactly where He told us to be and doing exactly what He told us to do. Ask the disciples who obeyed Christ's command to get in the boat and go to the other side of the Sea of Galilee. They were where Jesus told them to be and doing what He told them to do when they "fell into" a storm of massive proportions and feared for their very lives. Jesus came, walked on the water, stilled the disciples' storm, and strengthened their faith.

Yes, stress is predictable: all of us will experience it. None of us is immune to trials. Paul said these stressful situations are "common to man" (1 Corinthians 10:13). Clearly, it's not nearly as essential to try to explain trials philosophically or even theologically as it is for us to simply learn to deal with them. Once we realize stress is predictable—as in unavoidable—we can learn to deal with it, as James will teach us in the following chapters. Trials are *when*, not *if*. Stress happens to all of us. It is predictable.

JUST DO IT! So you find yourself a bit stressed? Don't be surprised. James just tapped you on the shoulder to remind you that stress can't be avoided. After all, stress is *when*, not *if*. Stress can bring emotional, mental, and physical problems as well as spiritual challenges if we do not recognize that stress is predictable and learn to deal with it. The battle is often in the mind, rooted in our surprise that life is hard. If you think you're going to live a stress-free life, you're mistaken. See the stress of life for what it is. God is allowing it. So "count it all joy."

3   STRESS IS PROBLEMATIC

My brethren, count it all joy when you fall into various trials.
—JAMES 1:2

*T*rials—and the stress they bring—are predictable: all of us will encounter them. And stress from trials can be problematic. In fact, it can be one of your worst enemies. It has ruined many lives and relationships. Stress hurts. It has cost some people their health, and others, their happiness.

Yet James said to consider "various trials" to be "all joy." James's term for *various trials* is an interesting word in the Greek language. The phrase can be literally translated as *many-colored trials.*

James knew that not all trials are alike and that we all react to stress in different ways. In other words, both our trials and our reactions come in many colors. Some people's response to stress is purple: they allow stress to so beat them up that they come out bruised and battered. Others' responses are blue: these people allow stress to move them into a state of depression where they just downright feel blue. Others respond to stress with the color green: they see others living seemingly carefree lives and become green with envy. Still others deal with stress with the color red: stress so builds up within them that they react with rage and anger toward those around them. Then there are those whose dealings with stress are yellow: they simply retreat in cowardice into their own little world. And some deal with stress with the color black: for them, everything in their experience becomes dark.

James was reminding us that there are many different kinds of trials and different kinds of reactions to those trials. Some trials are natural: they result from sickness, accidents, disappointments, or other painful circumstances. These trials naturally occur because we live in fleshly bodies in a sinful world. Other trials are supernatural in origin: they come our way because of our faith. Peter reminded us to "not think it strange concerning the fiery trial which is to try you, as though some strange thing happened to you" (1 Peter 4:12). Often when we line up with Christ, we line up against the world system around us.

For whatever reason a trial comes and in whatever form, the stress it causes can be problematic. Insurance companies tell us that their top medical claims and prescriptions are for what are called "preventable diseases." These are the result of sedentary lifestyles and the obesity that often results from stress-induced eating. In other words, high levels of stress foster the tendency to overeat. Too many people today don't exercise or eat healthily, and the result is an open invitation to stress.

The human body is one of God's most amazing and miraculous creations, yet, as I stated earlier, life's trials release certain stress hormones such as adrenaline. These chemical secretions cause the heart to pump faster, producing what is called the "fight or flight response." In primitive days these chemical changes prepared the body to respond to a weapon-wielding enemy or to fend off attacks of wild beasts. This extra burst of energy and strength enables almost superhuman strength for lifting an automobile off someone in a time of emergency or enabling the child cornered by the schoolyard bully to come out swinging. Problems arise when we do not fight or flee and those chemicals are not released from our body—we are left to deal with lingering stressful physical issues.

Our body, however, provides several indicators or warning signs to help us recognize stress in our lives. There are physical signs: tension, headaches, sleeplessness, changes in appetite, and high blood pressure. There are behavioral signs: a loss of productivity, strained relationships, a struggle to concentrate, and compulsive behavior. There are also emotional signs: depression, fear of failure, withdrawal, and frustration. Finally, there are spiritual signs: difficulty focusing, lack of prayer or Bible reading, and loss of passion. The presence of these warning signs is proof positive that stress in your life has become problematic.

No one is immune to stress and the damage it can cause. Elijah—one of the mightiest men in all the Bible—offers a case study of the sources, symptoms, and solutions to a stress-filled life. Just a few verses after Elijah enjoyed God's great victory over the false god Baal on Mount Carmel, we find the prophet stressed out and fleeing for his very life (1 Kings 18 and 19).

The stress that came into Elijah's life had several *sources*. First, there was *forgetfulness*. He had just come from one of his greatest victories, and he thought yesterday's victories would suffice for today's commitment. Thus, forgetfulness became a source of Elijah's stress and depression. Another source of stress is *fear*. Fear is not an action we take; it is a reaction. So is faith. When the crisis comes and our lives are governed by circumstances, we react in fear. However, if our lives are governed by the Lord and our hearts are saturated with Scripture, then faith is the natural response.

Another source of Elijah's stress was *fatigue*. He had just spent hours confronting the false prophets on Carmel, and the emotional stress must have been unbelievable. In addition, he had to run from Jezebel all the way to Beersheba, a distance of over one hundred miles. Elijah was exhausted. Fatigue is one of the plagues of modern man today. It often keeps us from thinking clearly and making wise decisions.

Elijah's story illustrates not only sources of stress but *symptoms* as well. The first is *detachment*. Elijah isolated himself. And withdrawing is one of the more blatant symptoms of stress. Unfortunately, we too often treat symptoms instead of sources. We think we can climb out of our doldrums by just getting out and socializing, but those doldrums are a symptom of stress, not a source. Another symptom of too much stress is *despondency*. Elijah sat under a juniper tree completely stressed out, and he even contemplated suicide. After despondency came *defeat*, a feeling of worthlessness and self-deprecation. This feeling is followed by *deception*. Elijah's faulty thinking led him to believe he was the only living person still standing for God. But God quickly reminded Elijah that He had thousands who had not followed after the false gods of Baal. How easy it is for us when we become stressed not to think correctly!

The good news is that there are also *solutions* to our stress-filled lives. First, there are *practical* and *physical* solutions. The first thing Elijah did about his stress was to get some sleep and have a solid meal. Adequate sleep and proper eating can go a long way in enabling us to deal with stress. But the solution is not simply physical; it is also *personal*. God asked Elijah, "What are you doing here?" (1 Kings 19:9). I often wonder which word in this question God emphasized. Did He ask, "What are *you* doing here?" Elijah once had such courage, but now he cowered. Perhaps God asked, "What are you doing *here*?" Have you ever been in a place where you knew God didn't want you to be? Or maybe God said, "What are you *doing* here?" Many of us lose the joy of life by doing nothing. Whatever way God asked the question, Elijah heard that "still small voice" (1 Kings 19:12) calling him to new heights of faith. Our own stress does not have to be a dead end; it can simply be a turn in the road.

Although stress is problematic, there is hope because stress is transitory. On many pages of the Bible is a simple phrase: "And it came to pass." This stress, too, shall pass! After all, there hasn't been a sunset yet that hasn't been followed by a sunrise.

JUST DO IT! Stress is predictable,

and we all have to deal with it. It can wreak havoc on homes, hearts, and hopes when we don't deal with it properly. Although stress is problematic, we have a supernatural power within us. After all, we are the "temple of the Holy Spirit" (1 Corinthians 6:19). In the Old Testament, God had a temple for His people. Today He has people—you and me—as His temple, His dwelling place. God is in you and with you, and as you read these words, God may well be speaking to you in that same "still small voice" that Elijah heard. Stress may have its sources and symptoms, but the good news is, it also has its solutions. Start applying them today.

4   STRESS IS PARADOXICAL

My brethren, count it all joy when you fall into various trials, knowing that the testing of your faith produces patience. But let patience have its perfect work, that you may be perfect and complete, lacking nothing.

—JAMES 1:2–4

James insisted we should "count it all joy" when we face stressful trials of many different kinds. Count it *what*? Joy! And how much joy? All joy! Could this be a misprint? Most of us consider various kinds of trials a taste of hell itself, certainly not joy. We tend to count it all joy when we avoid trials, not when we fall into them. We hear of someone else's trial and breathe a prayer of joyful thanks that the same fate has not fallen to us. What a paradox then! We're to counter stress with joy? James's admonition seems diametrically opposed to the way we tend to look at life's challenges and difficulties. On the surface, this advice appears strange. Most of us would say, "Count it all joy when you *escape* trials of various kinds."

Dr. Peter Hanson, however, wrote a book with a title that captured my attention: *The Joy of Stress.* The major premise is that stress should not be looked upon as our enemy. We should let go of the misconception that we can avoid stress. We can't. It's a part of life. For those of us who believe in the supernatural power of Christ, our times of stress should be times of making sure we are in the will of God. Stress is actually rather neutral. The way we react to it is the issue. In the Sermon on the Mount (Matthew 5–7), Jesus preached about the importance of our reactions. Jesus said, for instance, when someone slaps us on the cheek, we are to "turn the other to him also" (Matthew 5:39). Or if someone wants to sue us for a piece of our clothing, we should give him our coat as well (v. 40). These are hard sayings, but dealing with stress is hard as well as counterintuitive and paradoxical. But we can, James insisted, deal with stress by learning to "count it all joy."

When James wrote these words, he placed the phrase "count it all joy" in a tense that indicates exactly when we are to do that counting: when the trial is in the rearview mirror, we can begin to count it joy. James wasn't saying the trial itself should be considered a joy. The word *consider* (sometimes translated *count*) literally means "to think ahead, to think forward." This is exactly what Job was doing when he said, "When [God] has tested me, I shall come forth as gold" (Job 23:10). Job did not at all consider losing his family, his wealth, and his health a joy, but he did look forward to the joy he knew would follow his trial.

Joseph is another spot-on example: he was always thinking ahead, looking beyond his trials. When revealing his identity to his brothers, he said, "You meant evil against me; but God meant it for good, in order to bring it about as it is this day"

(Genesis 50:20). Did Joseph "count it all joy" to be abandoned and sold by his own brothers? Did he "count it all joy" when he was falsely accused and put in an Egyptian prison? Of course not. But Joseph trusted in the Lord. He knew God's hand was in his circumstances, and he was thinking ahead to a better day.

And what about our Lord Himself? He definitely looked beyond His own painful circumstances and intense suffering. Hebrews 12:2 says that "for the joy that was set before Him [He] endured the cross, despising the shame, and has sat down at the right hand of the throne of God." Did Jesus count the cross a joy? Certainly not. But thinking ahead with steadfast hope, He bore up under the stress of the cross.

Can we like Job or Joseph or Jesus think ahead in the midst of our own less-than-ideal circumstances and stressful situations? James was not telling us to try to find some kind of superficial joy during life's trials. What James told us is to look beyond them, for "joy comes in the morning" (Psalm 30:5).

The apostle Paul hit the bull's-eye when he said,

> Our light affliction, which is but for a moment, is working for us a far more exceeding and eternal weight of glory, while we do not look at the things which are seen, but at the things which are not seen. For the things which are seen are temporary, but the things which are not seen are eternal. (2 Corinthians 4:17–18)

In his book *Can Stress Heal?* Dr. Kenneth Cooper devotes an entire section to the paradoxical nature of stress. He identifies seven steps to what he calls "stress immunization":

STEP 1: "Assume a paradoxical mind-set." *This is precisely what James said two thousand years ago: "Count it all joy when you fall into various trials."*

STEP 2: "Build a foundation of healthy sleep."

STEP 3: "Take regular doses of nature's best tranquilizer . . . physical exercise."

STEP 4: "Fight stress at the molecular level." *Consult your physician to rule out any chemical imbalances.*

STEP 5: "Erect a powerful mind-spirit defense perimeter." *A spiritual dimension is at play here.*

STEP 6: "Become an expert in using depressurizing tactics." *Get away. Get alone. Retreat. Jesus did.*

STEP 7: "Get regular medical stress checkups."

Back to James. He was addressing "my brethren" in verse 2, and this is significant. *Brethren* indicates those people who share values and beliefs. James was writing to his brothers and sisters in the faith. It is folly to tell a man without a spiritual life to count it joy when the trials come. James's approach to stress is a family secret. As we discovered in *The Joshua Code*, we who are God's children have a family secret: "We know that all things work together for good to those who love God, to those who are the called according to His purpose"

(Romans 8:28). The lost world doesn't know this truth. Note the first phrase of the verse again: "We know . . ."

Every stressful trial can become an opportunity for growing in the likeness of Jesus Christ. Roy Hession once wrote, "Every humiliation, everything that tries and vexes us, is God's way of cutting a deeper channel in us through which the life of Christ can flow."* Yes, stress has a paradoxical nature to it. James went on to say, "Knowing that the testing of your faith produces patience. But let patience have its perfect work, that you may be perfect and complete, lacking nothing" (James 1:3–4).

JUST DO IT! Almost all stressful trials of life are temporary. Also, most of the things I worried about over the course of my life never even happened. And those that did passed by after time. Yes, go ahead. Count your trials all joy!

*Roy Hession, *The Calvary Road* (Fort Washington, PA: Christian Literature Crusade, 1964), p 154.

5   STRESS IS PURPOSEFUL

The testing of your faith produces patience. But let patience have its perfect work, that you may be perfect and complete, lacking nothing. If any of you lacks wisdom, let him ask of God, who gives to all liberally and without reproach, and it will be given to him. But let him ask in faith, with no doubting, for he who doubts is like a wave of the sea driven and tossed by the wind. For let not that man suppose that he will receive anything from the Lord; he is a double-minded man, unstable in all his ways.

—JAMES 1:3–8

*J*ames next reminded us that stress is not simply predictable, problematic, and paradoxical. Stress is also purposeful. We can actually benefit from stress.

To be specific, stress can help produce *purity* in our lives. James spoke of the "testing" of our faith that happens in the process of stress. Simon Peter used the same word to say that various trials come our way so "that the genuineness of your faith, being much more precious than gold that perishes, though it is tested by fire, may be found to praise, honor, and glory at the revelation of Jesus Christ" (1 Peter 1:7). This same word is also translated *purging*. Picture a piece of precious metal being heated until it is liquid and its impurities rise to the top and are scraped off. Only pure metal remains. By using this word, James was indicating that our stressful trials are for a purpose. They have their own way of refining us.

Stress also has the purpose of producing *perseverance* in our lives. Peter said that this testing results in patience or perseverance. The word literally means "to stand up under." Only trials of our faith can prove the depth of our faith and the strength of our character. You may be in a time of testing and the heat is on. Know that there is a purpose in your trials. God is perfecting you, enabling you to "stand up under" whatever comes your way.

Another purpose of stress is to lead us to *perfection*: "that you may be perfect and complete, lacking nothing." The word *perfect* here means "to carry to its end, to become full grown, to mature." The word picture is of a student who goes to school to earn a diploma. Along the way he may miss a few math problems, fail a test or two, and confuse some historical facts. But all of that is incidental to finishing his studies and getting his degree. Our goal in Christian living is spiritual maturity. Tests come along the way, and they are there to bring us to fruition and maturity.

Stress can also prompt *prayer*: "If any of you lacks wisdom, let him ask of God." There is a difference between wisdom and knowledge. Knowledge is the accumulation of facts. Most all of us can grow in knowledge if we stay in the library long enough. Wisdom, however, is the ability to take the facts at hand and, using heavenly judgment, apply what we know to the earthly situations around us. This was the point of Paul's prayer for the church at Ephesus. Paul asked "that the God of our Lord Jesus Christ, the Father of glory, may give to you the spirit of wisdom" (Ephesians 1:17). It was also Paul's prayer for the Colossians: "We continually ask God to fill you with the knowledge of his will through all the wisdom and understanding that the Spirit gives" (Colossians 1:9 NIV). During stressful trials, we often have a tendency to lose perspective and direction. We need wisdom.

In our educated and sophisticated world, we need wisdom. The present generation is more progressive than all those before it. We travel farther and fly faster and higher. More young people have graduate degrees than ever before. Knowledge is exploding. We accumulate data in a way that would have been unfathomable to my father's generation. Technology advances so quickly that the latest and greatest computers are out-of-date a few months after their release.

Yes, knowledge is exploding, and tools for obtaining knowledge have become more advanced, but wisdom is clearly lacking. Families are broken. Lives are in shambles. Suicide rates are higher than ever. Evidence of Christian morality is at a record low. Our world is dark and violent, constantly on the brink of one chaotic episode after another. Wisdom is lacking, but—as James said—"If any of you lacks wisdom, let him ask of God."

To whom does God give divine discernment? To those who *ask*. We don't get wisdom in school or from practical experience. Wisdom is God's gift to us. And His desire is to give it "liberally" when we ask. Yet many of us who need wisdom in

the midst of a stressful trial seem too proud to ask for it. We can learn about this from Solomon.

When the young King Solomon was about to begin ruling Israel, God presented him with an incredible proposition: "Ask! What shall I give you?" (1 Kings 3:5). And Solomon's request? "Give to Your servant an understanding heart to judge Your people, that I may discern between good and evil" (1 Kings 3:9). At that moment he could have asked for anything, and Solomon asked for wisdom—he knew he needed it.

Here is how life goes when we lack wisdom. The stressful crisis comes. We try to cope. We call the doctor to get another prescription. We make an appointment with our counselor. We order the latest self-help book. Do we think to bring the situation to the Lord and lay it at His feet in prayer? There is nothing wrong with those other approaches, but so often we consider prayer a last resort instead of the starting point for dealing with stress. As Psalm 118:8 says, "It is better to trust in the Lord than to put confidence in man."

James had more to say about prayer at this point. How we ask is important: "Let him ask in faith, with no doubting, for he who doubts is like a wave of the sea driven and tossed by the wind. For let not that man suppose that he will receive anything from the Lord." (James 1:6–7). Not everyone who asks for wisdom receives it. Wisdom is granted to those who believe, who ask in faith. Jesus put it thus: "Whatever things you ask when you pray, believe that you receive them, and you will have them" (Mark 11:24). And where do we find this faith? From the Bible. "Faith comes by hearing, and hearing by the word of God" (Romans 10:17). The prayer prayed in faith is born of the word when the Holy Spirit quickens our hearts. Prayer without the truths from the Bible has no direction, and the Bible unaccompanied by prayer lacks dynamic.

The person who lives with doubt in times of stressful trials is "double-minded . . . unstable in all his ways" (James 1:8). The doubter is trying to serve two masters. A part of him shouts, "I believe!" and another whispers, "I doubt." James said this type of person is "unstable in all his ways," resulting in increased stress instead of any stress relief.

Stress can actually be purposeful to those who dare to become vulnerable and accountable to God. What is our greatest need in times of stress? Wisdom for how to deal with the issues of life. How do we get wisdom? We ask for it. Who gives it? Our great Creator God who sees when a sparrow falls and cares much more about you. When does He give it? When we ask in believing prayer, for "without faith it is impossible to please Him" (Hebrews 11:6). How will He give it? Liberally.

Finally, King David's Psalm 111 adds to the discussion: "The fear of the LORD is the beginning of wisdom" (v. 10). The man or woman who has no reverence for God lacks true wisdom. He or she may be highly intelligent and have accumulated a multitude of facts, but no wisdom. Wisdom does not come from Plato or Aristotle or Socrates or Kierkegaard, or any other philosopher. Look again at the true source of wisdom and go ahead! "Ask of God!"

JUST DO IT! We have a God who cares about us. He is willing and able to fill us with His power and presence during life's trials. Try it. Just take Him at His word. Call on Him. He delights in making a way out of what seems inescapable.

Let the lowly brother glory in his exaltation, but the rich in his humiliation, because as a flower of the field he will pass away. For no sooner has the sun risen with a burning heat than it withers the grass; its flower falls, and its beautiful appearance perishes. So the rich man also will fade away in his pursuits. Blessed is the man who endures temptation; for when he has been approved, he will receive the crown of life which the Lord has promised to those who love Him.

—JAMES 1:9–12

It has been said that a Christian is like a tea bag: he is not worth much until he has been through some hot water. And hot water—stressful trials—can be profitable to the believer. James illustrated this fact with his descriptions of the person with poverty, the person with plenty, and the person with pressure. Trials have a way of bringing all of us to the same level of need. They knock on the door of the little frame home with iron bars on the windows in the transitional neighborhood as well as on the door of the multimillion-dollar waterfront home behind the big iron gates.

Take the person with poverty. James said, "Let the lowly brother glory in his exaltation." James described here a person who is low on the socioeconomic level, relatively poor, and powerless. While the world might think little of him, God thinks much of him. Here is one of the mysteries of God's economy: the last shall be first, and the low shall be made high in God's sight. James encouraged this believing person to take pride in his high position. As a follower of Christ, he is of great worth to God and can rejoice in the spiritual things he can never lose. Jim Elliot, the missionary martyred by the Auca Indians, left us these words in his diary: "He is no fool who gives what he cannot keep to gain what he cannot lose."* The apostle Paul reminded us that "our citizenship is in heaven, from which we also eagerly wait for the Savior, the Lord Jesus Christ" (Philippians 3:20).

James then turned his attention to the person with plenty. A beautiful thing about the church is that it is made up of all people. The early church was blessed with men of wealth such as Joseph of Arimathea, Nicodemus, and Barnabas. People blessed with material possessions may take pride in them, but Christians know that earthly treasures will one day rust, rot, or be devoured by moths. Poverty and plenty are temporary. No matter how much you have, someone else has more; no matter how little you have, someone else has less. Neither poverty nor plenty make for happiness in the Christian life. As Jesus taught, "One's life does not consist in the abundance of the things he possesses" (Luke 12:15). Those with plenty as well as those with poverty should rejoice in the spiritual things they cannot lose.

Another beautiful thing about the gospel is its leveling effect. In Jericho, Jesus and His disciples met two men on the same day. One was a man in poverty, the other a man with plenty. To Bartimaeus, the poverty-stricken blind beggar sitting on the side of the road, Jesus said, "Rise!" (Mark 10:49). To Zacchaeus, the wealthy tax collector perched in the tree, Jesus said, "Come down!" (Luke 19:5). What a picture of James's point: the gospel has a leveling effect.

Switching his focus a bit, James wrote: "Blessed is the man who endures temptation; for when he has been approved, he will receive the crown of life which the Lord has promised to those who love Him" (James 1:12). Satan attempts to use our stressful trials to cause us to stumble, but the Lord allows them in order to strengthen our faith muscles so we can stand strong. James chose the word *endures* to indicate staying power. Here is a man who holds his ground and stands up under life's stressful trials: he endures.

"Blessed"—happy—is the person who endures under stressful trials. Why? Because he knows that after the trial he will receive the "crown of life." In the ancient Grecian games, a wreath was placed on the head of the victor as a sign of honor and triumph. This is the very crown the apostle Paul had in mind when, in some of the last words he wrote before being martyred, he said,

> I have fought the good fight, I have finished the race, I have kept the faith. Finally, there is laid up for me the crown of righteousness, which the Lord, the righteous Judge, will give to me on that Day, and not to me only but also to all who have loved His appearing. (2 Timothy 4:7–8)

God has a special reward for those patient sufferers who endure their stressful trials. They win in the end.

Echoing the theme of James 1:12, the apostle John later recorded these words from the lips of our Lord: "Do not fear any of those things you are about to suffer. Indeed, the devil is about to throw some of you into prison, that you may be tested, and you will have tribulation ten days. Be faithful until death, and I will give you the crown of life" (Revelation 2:10). No wonder Fanny Crosby, who herself endured the stress of a lifetime of blindness, said:

> Great things He has taught us, great things He hath done,
> And great our rejoicing through Jesus the Son;
> But purer, and higher, and greater will be
> Our wonder, our transport, when Jesus we see.[1]

A little boy once found a cocoon attached to a small branch of a tree. He took the branch home and kept it in his room. When spring came, he watched as the emerging butterfly began its struggle to escape from its prison. Wanting to help, the boy found a pair of small scissors and made a slight incision in the side of the cocoon. Soon the butterfly emerged in all its glory—but it never flew! Having avoided all the struggle of having to emerge from the cocoon, the butterfly's wings never properly developed. The boy's good intentions actually robbed the butterfly of its ability to soar. In James's own words, "Let patience have its perfect work, that you may be perfect and complete, lacking nothing" (James 1:4).

Stress is a menace of modern man. It is predictable: it is a question of *when*, not *if*, and it's not going away. It is problematic: left ignored, it can be physically, emotionally, and spiritually destructive. It is paradoxical: we can count it joy knowing that the outcome will be for our good and His glory. It is purposeful: the stress we now feel is there for a God-allowed purpose. It is often a time of testing, of stripping ourselves of false priorities. And it is profitable. Just think ahead: we win in the end.

JUST DO IT! Stress provides us an incredible opportunity to identify with Christ. No one ever lived under more stressful conditions. He knew family stress: His own brothers disowned Him for a while and accused Him of being deranged. He knew the stress of having His friends desert Him in His time of greatest need. Then came the stress of the cross when He was forsaken by the Father (Matthew 27:46) so we might never be forsaken. Jesus was constantly misunderstood, falsely accused, cruelly beaten, and ultimately executed, only to return from the grave, the living Lord victorious over sin and death. Stress may be inevitable, but it can also be profitable.

*"To God Be the Glory" https://www.hymnal.net/en/hymn/h/39

7 RELATIVISM: *The* RELIGION *of* CONTEMPORARY CULTURE

Let no one say when he is tempted, "I am tempted by God"; for God cannot be tempted by evil, nor does He Himself tempt anyone. But each one is tempted when he is drawn away by his own desires and enticed. Then, when desire has conceived, it gives birth to sin; and sin, when it is full-grown, brings forth death. Do not be deceived, my beloved brethren. Every good gift and every perfect gift is from above, and comes down from the Father of lights, with whom there is no variation or shadow of turning.

—JAMES 1:13–17

*J*ames's letter to the scattered believers of the first century is as up-to-date with the issues facing modern man as any best-selling book in the marketplace. In the paragraph before us, James addressed the subject of relativism—which is sweeping the Western world in this third millennium.

The prophets of this religion preach that morality exists only in relation to the present culture, that is, within its historical and societal context. Thus, there is no room for anything as archaic as long-standing moral absolutes. The relativist argues that all truth claims are valid regardless of their origin or outcome. This philosophy creates a world in which nothing is necessarily wrong and where there are no right or wrong answers to any issues of life. Justice and fairness are not high-level concerns, resulting in no accountability and little, if any, tolerance for real moral discourse. In the mind of the relativist, the end result is that evil does not exist. In fact, in his bestselling 1987 *The Closing of the American Mind,* Professor Allan Bloom noted that our inability to recognize and identify evil would be a sign that our society is in grave danger. He has been proven to be a prophet in our time.

We live in a culture not unlike the one James addressed. Our world and our educational systems are becoming void of any discussion of moral absolutes. We bow before a myriad of little gods of our own making. The Ten Commandments are viewed as out-of-date and out of touch even though they have served as the basic building block of every decent democracy in history. We should not be surprised by repeated efforts to have the Ten Commandments removed from our schools and wiped off our national monuments. Simply put, relativism actually redefines—in the words of a former president—what the meaning of "is" is.

Morality is a forgotten concept in our culture. Few people ever think about, much less speak of, temptation anymore. Premarital sex is a virtual given. Relativism, this religion of modern man that offers a life with no moral absolutes, is our culture's chosen altar of worship. Consequently, as the front pages of our newspapers attest in one way or another almost every day, there are basically no restraints on words, actions, or relationships in the twenty-first century.

Major moral scandals frequently surface in every field of endeavor. Well-known athletes boast of illicit sex with hundreds of different partners. Others have been caught gambling large sums on their own teams. At one point in our past, presidential hopefuls would drown in the murky waters of immorality. But today politicians talk of smoking dope in their younger years, and some are known for having multiple adulterous affairs, but no behavior—past or present—has any real political consequences. High-level business executives, who thought they were above the law, have found themselves in lowly prison cells rather than lofty penthouses. And let's be honest: too many leaders in the Christian faith have been exposed for unsavory double standards.

Clearly, James's words about temptation in 1:13–17 have never been more appropriate or more applicable than in today's moral—or amoral—climate. James's caution speaks to our own culture: "Do not be deceived, my beloved brethren" (v. 16). Having addressed external trials earlier in this letter, James then turned his attention to internal temptations. The same Greek word translated in its noun form as "trials" in verse 2 is translated in its verb form as "tempted" in verse 13. The context of these words provides for us the key to understanding their difference. As we previously observed, James was discussing the testing of our faith. He said, "Count it all joy when you fall into various trials" (v. 2). Now he switched gears to highlight our propensity to sin: "Let no one say when he is tempted, 'I am tempted by God'" (v. 13).

While the very idea of temptation may not exist for proponents of relativism, it is the very heart of James's words in the paragraph before us (vv. 13–17). Beginning at the root, James spoke first about the *cause* of temptation: it has an internal source. Next, James revealed its *course*: like all weeds, temptation has a root (a selfish desire), a shoot (a sinful decision), and a fruit (a sure defeat). Finally, James gave a *caution* about dealing with temptations that come our way. He warned us not to be deceived about our sin, about our Savior, or about our salvation.

From time to time we all find our way to temptation's corner and must make decisions about which way to go. The light turns green. Horns honk. And too many of us make wrong and sometimes costly turns under such conditions . . . unless we have already decided which way to turn before we get to the intersection.

JUST DO IT! Don't believe the false religion of relativism. There are today—and there always have been—moral absolutes in life. We need these boundaries. After all, when is a train most free—when it is running on its tracks or when it is off the tracks? On another front, all truth claims are not valid. Since "faith comes by hearing, and hearing by the word of God" (Romans 10:17), let's hear and heed what James said not just to a first-century world but also to our contemporary culture today. James gave us some valuable instruction about which way to turn so that we can be strong *before* we even get to temptation's intersection. Read on.

8   *The* CAUSE *of* TEMPTATION

*Let no one say when he is tempted, "I am tempted by God";
for God cannot be tempted by evil, nor does He Himself tempt
anyone. But each one is tempted when he is drawn away by his
own desires and enticed.*

—JAMES 1:13–14

mong the many things we all have in common is that
temptation knocks on each of our doors. But where
does it come from? Is it from God? Is it from the Devil? Does
it simply arise out of circumstances swirling around us?

Some people are quick to attribute temptation to God
Himself. After all, the argument goes, since He created everything, it stands to reason that the tempting item or situation
as well as the impulse within us to succumb must ultimately
come from Him, so He is ultimately responsible. This line of
thinking leads to the rationale, "I can't help it. God made me
this way."

The Greek word James used to say that God "cannot be
tempted" appears only here in the New Testament. It literally
translates "untemptable." Since He is not guilty of sin, He cannot tempt us toward it. Satan figured wrong with his efforts to
tempt Jesus in the wilderness. Not one of his enticements met

with any success. Jesus, in fact, knew no sin (2 Corinthians 5:21; Hebrews 4:15; 1 John 3:5). Therefore, James flatly said, "Let no one say when he is tempted, 'I am tempted by God'" (1:13).

From the garden of Eden until this present day, men and women have tried to avoid personal responsibility by blaming their sin on the Devil. "The Devil made me do it!" started way back in the garden when Adam said, "Don't blame me! The woman dragged me down." Eve fired back, "Not me! The Devil made me do it." Not true! We inherited this tendency to sin from Adam and Eve.

Satan is not the cause of our temptations. James laid it out plainly: "Each one is tempted when he is drawn away *by his own desires*" (1:14, emphasis mine). In James's entire discussion on temptation, the Devil is never mentioned. In the garden of Eden, all the Devil did was toss an evil desire in Eve's direction, and she took it from there.

There are some people who readily admit it is not God's fault, or the Devil's, that we are tempted. Instead they argue, "It is just one of those things. We find ourselves in a situation where we shouldn't have been." But James made clear to us that neither God nor Satan nor circumstances brings us to temptation's corner.

What, then, is the cause? Temptation comes when an internal source and an external force converge: "Each one is tempted when he is drawn away by his own desires and enticed." When our internal desire to do wrong connects with a harmful outward enticement, we succumb to temptation. We sin.

AN INTERNAL SOURCE

James said that temptation begins when we are "drawn away by [our] own desires" (v. 14). However, not all desires are bad. The desire to eat and drink is good when kept within God's guidelines. The desire for rest and sleep is good within limits. And, within God's stated boundaries, the desire for sex is a good thing. The problem comes when we want to satisfy our desires outside of God's will. For example, eating is enjoyable, but gluttony is a sin. Sleep is essential, but slothfulness is a sin. Sexual relationships within the marriage covenant are healthy, but adultery is a sin. Many of our desires are not evil in and of themselves. But some of them are, and that means trouble.

When our "own desires" (the internal source of temptation) attach themselves to an evil object, we are "drawn away" from our place of security. James painted a picture of us living in a secure place, only to allow a desire contrary to God's will to draw us away from that place of security into the open where we become vulnerable to sin.

Such temptation to sin is a very personal matter—what tempts one person may not tempt the next person at all. Hence the words James carefully crafted: "each one" is drawn away. No one is immune to sinful desires, and each of us is responsible for our "own desires." We cannot blame God, the Devil, or circumstances. If there were no evil desire in our heart, there would be no temptation to sin. Yet this internal source seeks to draw us away and causes us to want to play outside of God's boundaries.

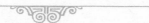

AN EXTERNAL FORCE

The internal source of temptation is selfish desire, the external force is deception; and when these two coincide, the result is sinful behavior.

James indicated that once desire becomes self-centered, it causes us to be "enticed." This word carries with it the connotation of being baited or deceived. The expression about being hooked on something finds its origin in this Greek word. And the mention of bait definitely calls for a fish story.

An eight-pound black bass I caught is the perfect illustration of both how temptation works and what happens when we don't heed James's warning. You see, I took a beautiful plastic worm, stuck a fishing hook through it, and bent the worm around the hook so it couldn't be seen. I attached a transparent fishing line to the hook. Then I dropped the worm into the lake and jiggled it along the bottom. From its hole the big bass saw this delicious-looking worm. It had a desire (an internal source), so when the external force came along, the bass could not resist. The bass swallowed the worm, was dragged away from its safe hole, and put into the boat where it met its demise.

All of us have been hooked by the world's allurements just as the bass was by my baited hook. Something, someone, some opportunity looked so attractive, so satisfying, so fulfilling. It was a complete deception, but we took the bait and got hooked. That fish would never have swum out of its hole to bite a bare hook. I had to hide it, disguise it, make it look attractive. Similarly, temptation appeals to our natural desires while deceptively hiding the fact that biting the worm, so to speak, will lead us to harm and destruction.

No one put the worm in the fish's mouth. It came out of the hole because of its own desire and took the bait. Sin doesn't start with the bait. Sin starts as a desire in our own hearts, and this has been true of human beings from the beginning. No one put the forbidden fruit in Eve's mouth. She desired the fruit even though she knew it was forbidden. Then came the external force of the serpent's word. She saw, she took, and the rest is history.

When we grab the bait, the hidden hook grabs us. Sin takes place when our selfish desire and Satan's deception connect, and we are lured away from our safe place in God's will. If it weren't for the evil desires within the human heart, Satan would never gain a victory when he dangles his enticing hooks in front of us. Sin does begin in the heart (Mark 7:20–23). What a person needs is a new nature, a change from within, a change of desires.

It is not a sin to be tempted. We are all tempted. Jesus Himself was tempted. Sin results when the internal source (self-centered desire) and the negative external force (deception) come together and we take the bait. Another example. Two men are walking down the street. They pass an enticement, a hooker. She smiles. They both see the bait. Why does one man take it and the other walk on by on the other side of the street? The men's responses are directly related to their internal desires. One has desires that abide within the parameter of God's will because he knows the Word and follows the Spirit. The other man has desires that are outside God's will because he has exposed himself to worldly or harmful influences.

On the evening before His crucifixion, while He agonized in prayer in Gethsemane's garden, Jesus left us some good advice when He said to His disciples, "Watch and pray, lest you enter into temptation" (Matthew 26:41). *Prayer* has to do with the internal source of temptation, our own desires. Prayer keeps us connected with God so that His desires are our desires. *Watching* has to do with the external force of temptation, the deception. We are to be alert, to watch out. The bait has a hook in it. If we look closely enough, we will see the enticement for what it is—a trap!

JUST DO IT! God is not the author of temptation. Nor is Satan. Nor is any situation. In our age of relativistic thinking—when individuals define their own morality—we who follow Jesus need to remember what God's Word teaches. The root of our temptation lies within us. James was shouting at us, "Do not be deceived!" (James 1:16).

9   *The* Course *of* Temptation

When desire has conceived, it gives birth to sin; and sin, when it is full-grown, brings forth death.

—JAMES 1:15

*S*alvation not only has its own cause; it also runs its own course. Sin leads us where we do not want to go, steers us toward defeat, and ultimately ends in death.

Temptation is like a weed growing in the midst of flowers in a garden: left unchecked it takes over. Now, as I stated in chapter 7, a weed has three distinct features. It has a root, a shoot, and a fruit. Left alone, the root produces a shoot that bursts forth out of the ground and immediately produces a fruit that, in turn, produces more weeds. This is exactly what James was describing in the verse before us. The evil desires within us "conceive" (they take root), then they "give birth to sin" (they shoot up), and finally they become "full-grown" (they produce a dangerous fruit).

The root of temptation is a selfish desire, the shoot is a sinful decision, and the resulting fruit is a sure defeat. Or, as James put it, "When desire has conceived, it gives birth to sin; and sin, when it is full-grown, brings forth death." And a law of Scripture is as certain and sure as the law of gravity.

THE ROOT: A SELFISH DESIRE

The word *desire* means "a strong urge, a craving of the soul." There is nothing inherently wrong with desire. In fact, desires can be productive and beneficial when we satisfy them within the laws God prescribed for our well-being. But here James was dealing with selfish desires, those that crop up in our minds and hearts.

As we saw in the preceding chapter, when the internal source (desire) and the external force (deception) come together, sin is conceived. The word translated into our English word *conceive* means "to bring together." So how does this bringing together happen? When we begin to desire something outside of God's boundaries and we take the bait when it comes by, conception takes place, and sin has taken root. Sin grows and at some point bursts out into the open.

When a selfish desire enters the mind and takes root, we should remove it immediately. If we don't, that desire will—like a weed—eventually produce fruit. To remove those thoughts the very moment one passes through your mind, immediately surrender your mind to Christ. Pray, "Lord, my mind is Yours, and my heart is Yours. Please put Your thoughts in me." If possible, open the Bible and feed on God's thoughts.

THE SHOOT: A SINFUL DECISION

Left alone, the root of selfish desire will inevitably give way to the shoot of a sinful decision. Sin is the result of a selfish desire left unchecked and our deliberate choice to act on that desire.

James said this desire eventually "gives birth to sin." This Greek phrase suggests a child in the mother's womb before making his appearance into the world. The evil desire cannot stay hidden within forever, any more than a child can stay in a mother's womb indefinitely. That desire will, for sure, "give birth." If the root of sin is left untouched in the heart, the shoot will emerge sooner or later. As the Bible says, "Your sin will find you out" (Numbers 32:23).

In James's words, our internal desire "gives birth to sin." The Greek behind the English word *sin* means "to miss the mark." The ancient Greek writers used this word in primarily three ways. In the physical dimension, it describes an archer who aims at the target, lets go of the arrow, and misses the bull's-eye. In the mental dimension, the word for sin describes a student who takes a test and fails to get the answers right. In the spiritual dimension, the word describes a person who knows a certain standard of behavior, yet falls below it. All of these individuals miss the mark.

Perhaps the most direct definition of sin is found in the Bible: "Sin is lawlessness" (1 John 3:4). Sin is the natural result of an evil desire left untouched. If a selfish desire is the root, then a sinful decision is certainly the shoot.

THE FRUIT: A SURE DEFEAT

There is an obvious progression here. First there is conception,

and then a stage of growth followed by a birth. But note carefully what James said about this birth: this sin "brings forth death!" It is stillborn!

James's warning to us was to look ahead to where our sin is leading us. Paul was a bit more blunt: "The wages of sin is death" (Romans 6:23). Ever since the garden of Eden, physical death has been the destiny of every human being. But the wages of sin can also mean the death of dreams, relationships, ambitions, reputations, opportunities, and so much else that is good. Sin never brings anything good into our lives.

In this verse *death* means "separation." In physical death, the spirit is separated from the body. In eternal death, the spirit of man is separated from God for all eternity. James was shouting at us, "Sin—when it is full-grown—gives birth to separation from all that is good! Wake up!"

When we take the bait, most of us never think of the possible consequences. Sin separates us from so much that is good and, all too often, results in the death of hopes, health, homes, and happiness.

We don't have to read far in the Bible before coming to the most glaring and obvious proof of the costly toll temptation takes when it leads to sin. Adam and Eve's fall began with their *selfish desire* to eat the forbidden fruit. It continued with their *sinful decision* to take it and eat. And it ended with a *sure defeat*: Adam and Eve were expelled from the garden. They experienced separation from God.

So, how should we deal with temptation, its cause, and its course? Most often, we should deal with temptation in the same way we deal with weeds in our garden. We can't only deal with the fruit: we cut off the tops of the weeds, but in a few days the weeds are back. Similarly, dealing with the fruit—saying, "We'll just stop sinning"—addresses only the externals. Another option is mowing the weeds all the way down to the ground, cutting off the shoots. The garden looks good and weed-free for a while.

The only effective way to deal with temptation is at its root. Let God pull out our sinful desires. He must change our desires and give us a new nature. The spiritually victorious life is an *ex*changed life, not merely a changed life. We give God our old life, and He will give us a brand-new life.

Let's consider from this perspective why Satan failed so miserably in his attempts to lure Christ into temptation. He wiggled the bait in front of our Lord. The external force was there, but there was no evil desire in the heart of Christ. The Lord Jesus never considered taking Satan's bait because Jesus kept His desires in line with the Father's desires. Jesus answered all three wilderness temptations the same way: with the Word of God, saying, "It is written" (Matthew 4:4, 7, 10). We, too, need to know and use the Word of God in our own encounters with temptation.

Do you see that the battlefield is the mind and heart? This is why Paul repeatedly said things like "Set your mind on things above, not on things on the earth" (Colossians 3:2) and "Whatever things are true, whatever things are noble, whatever things are just, whatever things are pure, whatever things are lovely, whatever things are of good report, if there is any virtue and if there is anything praiseworthy—meditate on these things" (Philippians 4:8). Allowing our minds to think on impure things is dangerous and downright damaging. After all, those thoughts are the root of all sin.

One more thought about temptation. The first verse of Scripture I ever memorized was one I have quoted to myself thousands of times across the years: "No temptation has overtaken you except such as is common to man; but God is faithful, who will not allow you to be tempted beyond what you are able, but with the temptation will also make the way of escape, that you may be able to bear it" (1 Corinthians 10:13).

JUST DO IT! Think about a hotel. The manager cannot keep someone from coming into the lobby, but he can keep that person from getting a room. Your mind is like a hotel. It isn't a sin when an impure thought passes through your mind. It becomes a sin when you don't allow it to pass through and instead give it a room in your heart. Stand strong in the Lord and against temptation. Keep in mind that "[God] will not allow you to be tempted beyond what you are able" (1 Corinthians 10:13).

10 *The* CAUTION ABOUT TEMPTATION

Do not be deceived, my beloved brethren. Every good gift and every perfect gift is from above, and comes down from the Father of lights, with whom there is no variation or shadow of turning.

—JAMES 1:16–17

*J*ames concluded his words about temptation with a flashing yellow caution light designed to get our attention: "Don't be deceived!" In other words, "Don't get off course or go in the wrong direction." The Greek word we translate *deceived* describes a ship that strays from its designated route. Remember that James was writing to believers, to his "beloved brethren." It is possible for us to be deceived and get off course. That's why James warned us not to be deceived about three specific things.

DON'T BE DECEIVED ABOUT SIN

The truth is, many of us are deceived about sin. Today's secular academia looks at sin as an archaic concept. In our age of widespread unbelief, with few restraints on behavior and an almost universal cultural acceptance that no real moral absolutes exist, we should not be surprised that many people end up doing "what [is] right in his own eyes" (Judges 21:25). But while our culture tells us, "If it feels good, do it," James was cupping his hands to his mouth and calling to us across the centuries, "Do not be deceived!"

We in the Western world have raised a couple of generations who have few, if any, absolutes. Relativism guides their thought processes, so it is increasingly difficult to convince them that sin exists. Consider sex as an example. It is God's beautiful and special gift to us. However, used wrongly, sex has a destructive and often debilitating effect on those involved. Most people don't realize that sexual sin is different from all other sin. It is the sole sin a person commits not only against God but against himself or herself as well (1 Corinthians 6:18). Furthermore, our bodies are the temple, the dwelling place, of the Holy Spirit (v. 19). In Old Covenant times, God had a temple for His people. But, in our dispensation of grace, God has a people for His temple. You—your very body—is His dwelling place. Do not be deceived about sin. Keep pure for Him.

DON'T BE DECEIVED ABOUT THE SAVIOR

"Every good gift and every perfect gift is from above, and comes down from the Father of lights" (James 1:17). God is the Author of all that is good. He is not the cause of sin or of suffering. So don't be deceived: anything and everything good comes from God alone.

James spoke of the good and perfect "gifts" that come from

above. The value of a gift, however, can be diminished by the way it is given. If someone simply tosses a gift in your direction as though she were simply fulfilling some obligation, that action would take away some of the joy of receiving it. When God gives gifts, He always does so in a loving way.

James reminded us that our "Father of lights" does not change like some shifting shadow. Life may have its shadows, but they are never caused by God's turning away. Don't be deceived about the light and love of your Savior, Jesus Christ. There is no "shadow of turning" with Him.

Yes, that phrase appears in the classic hymn "Great Is Thy Faithfulness." Throughout the years, one of my great joys has been repeating hymns of praise to the Father. I suppose this is the stanza I have prayed the most:

> Great is Thy faithfulness, O God, my Father;
> There is no shadow of turning with Thee;
> Thou changest not, Thy compassions, they fail not;
> As Thou hast been, Thou forever wilt be.
> Great is Thy faithfulness! Great is Thy faithfulness!
> Morning by morning new mercies I see.
> All I have needed Thy hand hath provided;
> Great is Thy faithfulness, Lord, unto me!*

DON'T BE DECEIVED ABOUT SALVATION

The only way to have victory over temptation and sin is to know Christ personally. When you confess your sin, accept God's forgiveness, and acknowledge Jesus as His Son and your Savior and Lord, you receive a new nature, a God-given nature. Remember that the Devil never gives such good gifts. His gifts may look quite enticing, but they have hooks in them. James was calling upon us not to be deceived by the Devil's bait. God alone offers the good gift of salvation, and He offers it to any and all who ask and receive. Again, "every good gift and every perfect gift is from above, and comes down from the Father of lights" (1:17).

It is important to note that the gift of salvation is "from above." Jesus called salvation the "new birth" because, among other ways salvation impacts our lives, salvation changes our desires. Salvation causes old things to go away and new things to come into our lives (2 Corinthians 5:17). When I acknowledged my sin, asked God to forgive me, stated my belief in His death and resurrection, and placed my entire trust in Him, He came into my life. Although decades later I am still not the person I want to be, I haven't been the same since that day. When Christ took up residence in my life, I immediately began to love what I used to hate and hate what I used to love. Things I used to like to do and places I used to like to go held no attraction anymore. And things I never thought I'd like to do—like read a Bible or fellowship in a church—became my new passion. Only God can give a good gift like that.

Maybe you know the song "Tie a Yellow Ribbon Round the Ole Oak Tree." It tells the story of a young man going home from prison who wondered if his love wanted him back. He told her of the appointed day of his return and asked that if he was welcome, she would tie a single yellow ribbon on the oak tree in the front yard. If he saw the ribbon, he would go in; if he didn't, he would start life anew somewhere else. When he came down the street, he saw to his delight "a hundred yellow ribbons" on that oak tree.

Some of us who have wandered off course may, like that young man, want to go back home and begin again. If that's true for you, know that God has tied His own red ribbon around Calvary's tree. Know, too, that "the blood of Jesus Christ His Son cleanses us from all sin."

JUST DO IT!

Temptation has its own cause, temptation takes its own course, and God offers His own caution to us all. First, "don't be deceived" about sin. We can't minimize our sin by saying it's not as bad as other people's sin, and we can't dismiss our sin by saying that everyone else is doing it. Sin—any and all sin—is so serious that it required Jesus to die on the cross. Second, don't be deceived about salvation. We are saved not because of our own good works or heartfelt efforts, but entirely by God's grace when we simply put our faith in Christ (Ephesians 2:8–9). And, finally, don't be deceived about our Savior. Jesus was not merely another prophet or teacher or religious leader. He was God who came in human flesh and paid the penalty for our sin on a cross. Then He rose from the grave on the third day, victorious over sin and death! No wonder James said, "Every good gift and every perfect gift is from above, and comes down from the Father of lights, with whom there is no variation or shadow of turning" (1:17).

*https://www.hymnal.net/en/hymn/h/19

11 *The* CREDIBILITY CRISIS

Of His own will He brought us forth by the word of truth, that we might be a kind of firstfruits of His creatures. So then, my beloved brethren, let every man be swift to hear, slow to speak, slow to wrath; for the wrath of man does not produce the righteousness of God. Therefore lay aside all filthiness and overflow of wickedness, and receive with meekness the implanted word, which is able to save your souls. But be doers of the word, and not hearers only, deceiving yourselves. For if anyone is a hearer of the word and not a doer, he is like a man observing his natural face in a mirror; for he observes himself, goes away, and immediately forgets what kind of man he was. But he who looks into the perfect law of liberty and continues in it, and is not a forgetful hearer but a doer of the work, this one will be blessed in what he does. If anyone among you thinks he is religious, and does not bridle his tongue but deceives his own heart, this one's religion is useless. Pure and undefiled religion before God and the Father is this: to visit orphans and widows in their trouble, and to keep oneself unspotted from the world.

—JAMES 1:18–27

In the Western world the Christian faith is facing a credibility crisis. In our attempt to be contemporary and to creatively reach others with the good news about Jesus Christ, we have forgotten that our credibility matters.

The differences between the first-century church and today's church twenty centuries later can be summarized in two words: *influence* and *power*. The early church did not have enough *influence* to keep Peter out of prison, but the believers had enough *power* to pray him out. Today, few Christians seem to speak of the power of the Holy Spirit, yet they pride themselves on influence. Sadly, most of the influence they think they have is their perception, not reality.

How did the church in America get to this point? In the 1980s, the church stepped into the political arena and played a major part in electing Ronald Reagan as president of the United States. President Reagan brought renewed hope to our nation, and his policies prepared the way for some of America's finest hours. Ever so subtly, though, this political scene seemed to impact the church. With conservative Christianity being mentioned in front-page articles of daily newspapers and in lead stories on nightly news, the church began to flex its muscles. The church took pride in its newfound influence while confusing it with spiritual power. Not unexpectedly, the church soon found itself fighting for its own integrity and credibility. Denominations declined, and churches had scandal to rival Hollywood. Immorality and extravagance ran rampant behind closed church doors.

No wonder our world today is confused, needing to see a picture of genuine Christianity. As radical Islamic movements, Eastern mysticism, and a growing secularism gain momentum, it is becoming more and more imperative that God's church rises up in the power of the Holy Spirit, shows the world what lived-out Christianity is, and begins to make a difference once again.

"Pure . . . religion" (1:27) is the focus of James's words in the passage above. He revealed that true faith is characterized by three important factors: knowing Christ, sowing consistency, and showing character.

For many people religion is boring. It is for me! But Christianity is actually not about religion at all. It is about having a vital and vibrant, living and personal relationship with the Lord Jesus Christ.

So how can we influence our increasingly secular society? What can the church do to reach all generations including baby boomers who bought into the lie that people, possessions, position, and power bring peace and purpose to life? Although the boomers enjoyed more prosperity than any other generation, they also lead all other generations in such things as divorce, drug addiction, loneliness, and suicide. Clearly, our world needs a glimpse of true faith. To provide that, Christianity needs to be credible.

Let me repeat: Christianity is not about religion; it is about a relationship with Jesus. This is what distinguishes Christianity from all other world religions. Most other religions focus on man's quest to guarantee himself a place in heaven through good works, penance, almsgiving, and the like, all of which are feeble attempts by sinful humans to gain acceptance by a holy God. But Christianity is not about man

trying to get to God. It is about God coming down to us in the person of Jesus. Religion will never be able to change our world. It is, to this very day, at the root of most of the world's wars and conflicts. The hope of our world is not in religion of any kind. Real hope rests in a relationship with Jesus Christ.

JUST DO IT! We experience relationships in three directions. First is the *outward* expression: we have relationships with people at home, in the neighborhood, at the office, and in the social arena. Second, each of us has a relationship with ourselves that some call self-worth or self-esteem, and that is the *inward* direction. Third, we have a relationship in an *upward* direction—and that is incredible! We have the capacity to enter into a relationship with God through Jesus Christ and to know Him with the intimacy a child knows a father. This capacity to be in relationship with our holy Creator is what separates us human beings from all the rest of creation.

So what is the significance of these three directions of relationship? We will never be properly related to each other (outward) until we are properly related to ourselves. Much of what happens in strained relations is simply a projection of what is really going on in our own lives (inward). But we will never be able to fully accept ourselves until we discover how valuable we are to God and enter into a personal relationship with Him through the Lord Jesus Christ (upward). At that point, empowered by the Holy Spirit, we Christians will be well on our way to solving our church's credibility crisis.

12   True Faith Involves Knowing Christ

Of His own will He brought us forth by the word of truth, that we might be a kind of firstfruits of His creatures.

—JAMES 1:18

Throughout Christian history, people have tried to pit James, with his emphasis on works, against Paul, with his emphasis on grace. Some reformers even went so far as to suggest that James's epistle is an "epistle of straw" that falsely promoted a works salvation. Nothing could be further from the truth. Before James ever talked about works in chapter 2, he made sure that all his readers understood that salvation is in Christ alone. In James 1:18 he wrote of salvation's origin, its operation, and its outcome.

SALVATION'S ORIGIN

Biblical salvation has its origin in a divine regeneration; salvation does not and cannot result from any human effort or good works. By God's "own will," as James said, He chose to give us birth, to bring us "forth by the word of truth." Salvation begins with God, not with us. We don't initiate it; God does. We didn't originate it; He did. We can't sustain it;

He can. Had God not chosen us, we never would have chosen Him. As Isaiah put it seven hundred years before Christ, "All we like sheep have gone astray; we have turned, every one, to his own way; and the Lord has laid on Him the iniquity of us all" (Isaiah 53:6).

Without Christ, we are *unresponsive* to the offer of salvation. We are "dead in trespasses and sins" (Ephesians 2:1). When a man is dead physically, he doesn't respond to physical stimuli. He feels no pain or heat. Similarly, people who are dead spiritually do not respond to spiritual stimuli. They are unresponsive. Without Christ, we are also *unperceptive*: the gospel "is veiled to those who are perishing . . . who do not believe" (2 Corinthians 4:3–4). Without Christ, we are *unteachable* as well: "The natural man does not receive the things of the Spirit of God, for they are foolishness to him; nor can he know them, because they are spiritually discerned" (1 Corinthians 2:14). Finally, without Christ we are *unrighteous.* King David reminded us all of this fact: "I was brought forth in iniquity, and in sin my mother conceived me" (Psalm 51:5).

So far, our spiritual situation is not looking too good for us. But here comes the good news. Since we can do nothing in and of ourselves to reach our holy God, He must do something. He must be the initiator of our salvation—and He is! According to James, God chose to give us life: "Of His own will He brought us forth by the word of truth." As our Lord Jesus Christ plainly put it, "You did not choose Me, but I chose you" (John 15:16). Paul added, "He chose us in Him before the foundation of the world" (Ephesians 1:4). The Bible is the story of God's love for His chosen people.

How does this work for us? The Bible says that God calls us to Himself (Romans 8:29–30). There are two calls, the outward call and the inward call. The church of the Lord Jesus Christ issues the outward call in various manners and through various ministries. But only the Spirit issues the inward call to the heart. God chooses to give us new birth, to bring us "forth by the word of truth."

Only this new birth can bring a person into a new life. Salvation does not find its origin in heredity. We don't acquire it through osmosis. It isn't brought about by winsomeness or persuasive preaching. The new birth originates with God. Salvation is God's work, not ours. A genuine walk of faith comes with knowing Christ and understanding that salvation has its origin in God.

SALVATION'S OPERATION

Our salvation comes by "the word of truth." Put differently, we are born again "through the word of God which lives and abides forever" (1 Peter 1:23). No one has ever been converted apart from God's Word. As Paul clearly stated, "Faith comes by hearing and hearing by the word of God" (Romans 10:17).

Conviction always precedes conversion in a Christian's life. God's Word cuts us "to the heart" (Acts 2:37). The Word of God reveals to us that we are sinners in need of salvation. God's Word also makes plain to us the way to eternal life. Salvation operates through "the word of truth."

The Word of God, living and written, is God's instrument of salvation. True faith involves knowing Christ as Savior and Lord, knowing that salvation has its very origin in the sovereignty of God, and knowing that salvation operates through the Bible, God's Word to us.

SALVATION'S OUTCOME

James reminds us that the outcome of our salvation is "that we might be a kind of firstfruits of His creatures" (James 1:18). The Word of God is the seed that brings forth fruit in our lives.

Jesus was making this very point when, to the inquiring Greeks, He said, "Unless a grain of wheat falls into the ground and dies, it remains alone; but if it dies, it produces much grain" (John 12:24). We think that death comes from life. But Jesus revealed just the opposite: life actually comes from death.

Imagine, for a minute, that you drop a grain of wheat into the earth and cover it with soil. That little grain corrodes and rots—it dies—and then releases its life germ. After a while a tiny blade pushes its way through the soil and reaches up toward the sun. Days pass, weeks pass, and the blade eventually becomes a full-grown plant producing hundreds of little seeds just like the one you planted. All of that energy and life was in a single, tiny grain of wheat. But, you couldn't see it . . . until the seed died. Then it produced a lot more grain just like itself, many other "firstfruits."

Now imagine for a moment that instead of dropping that

69

little grain of wheat in the ground, you drop it in your desk drawer. Leave it there for a few months. Then go back to the drawer and open it. The seed is still there, but "it remains alone" (John 12:24).

During His sojourn on earth, Jesus remained just like that little seed in your desk drawer: He produced no one like Himself. After spending three years preparing for Jesus' departure, the disciples argued among themselves about which of them should be the greatest in the coming kingdom. Then, on the night He needed them most, they all forsook Him and fled in the darkness. But what a difference in them after Jesus died, after He was planted in the earth and then came forth on the third day! No longer did Jesus "remain alone." He became the "firstborn among many brethren" (Romans 8:29). And these first-century believers—who were scattered among the nations and to whom James was writing his letter—were the first generation to trust in Christ as their promised Messiah. James called them the "firstfruits" in God's forever family.

Once we become a part of God's family, we, too, will bear fruit; and Jesus said that people will know His people "by their fruits" (Matthew 7:16). Individuals knowing Christ is the first step in solving the church's credibility crisis.

JUST DO IT!

My life verse comes from Paul's letter to the Galatians: "I have been crucified with Christ; it is no longer I who live, but Christ lives in me; and the life which I now live in the flesh I live by faith in the Son of God, who loved me and gave Himself for me" (Galatians 2:20). As the Lord hung on that cross, the crowd saw only one Man, but the Father saw you and me and all the others who would put their faith in Christ and be "crucified with Christ." Our part is to receive that salvation, understanding that it has its origin in God, not in us, that we learn about salvation through God's Word, and that our salvation results in good works.

13   TRUE FAITH INVOLVES SOWING CONSISTENCY

So then, my beloved brethren, let every man be swift to hear, slow to speak, slow to wrath; for the wrath of man does not produce the righteousness of God. Therefore lay aside all filthiness and overflow of wickedness, and receive with meekness the implanted word, which is able to save your souls. But be doers of the word, and not hearers only, deceiving yourselves. For if anyone is a hearer of the word and not a doer, he is like a man observing his natural face in a mirror; for he observes himself, goes away, and immediately forgets what kind of man he was. But he who looks into the perfect law of liberty and continues in it, and is not a forgetful hearer but a doer of the work, this one will be blessed in what he does.

—JAMES 1:19–25

True faith begins with knowing Christ, and it continues with sowing consistency in our lives. This consistency manifests itself in our talk and our walk, our conversation and our conduct. If we are to present to the world a credible picture of Christ, we must not only genuinely know Him; we must also be consistent in living in a way that honors Him.

CONSISTENT IN OUR TALK

One obvious mark of genuine Christianity is having one's conversation be consistent with biblical standards and Christian beliefs. James emphasized how important it is to say the right thing in the right way and to be "swift to hear" as well. Consistency in talk for James meant that we actually listen more than we speak. He called upon us to be "swift to hear [and] slow to speak" (James 1:19). He didn't say we shouldn't speak, but that we should think before we speak. (I don't think it's any coincidence God gave us two ears and only one mouth. He could be subtly telling us to listen twice as much as we speak.)

Too often too many of us reverse James's order. We are often slow to listen and quick to speak. And problems result: "In the multitude of words sin is not lacking, but he who restrains his lips is wise" (Proverbs 10:19). Jesus warned that "every idle word men may speak, they will give account of it in the day of judgment. For by your words you will be justified and by your words you will be condemned" (Matthew 12:36–37). Credible Christian living demands we be cautious in our conversation and that our words are consistent with God's Word and character.

James admonished us to also be "slow to wrath," to "lay aside all filthiness and overflow of wickedness," and to "receive with meekness the implanted word, which is able to save your souls." Although God chooses us and calls us to Himself, there is something for us to do: we are to take off our old coats of sin and strip away all filth. This is not a requirement for salvation, since only the blood of Christ can cleanse us of sin. James was writing to believers like you and me who already know Christ. Knowing and therefore representing Jesus, these people need to be consistent in their conversation as well as their conduct. James did not back down: if we are going to show the world a credible Christ, then we must know Christ and sow consistency in our lives—beginning with our talk.

CONSISTENT IN OUR WALK

We now come to some of James's most famous and most often repeated words: "Be doers of the word, and not hearers only." Then comes a promise: he who "is not a forgetful hearer but a doer of the work, this one will be blessed in what he does." As a pastor for several years, I would rather see my people *do* one sermon than *hear* a hundred of them.

The desire to have my congregation *do* one sermon is supported by a process we have all experienced many times. How did you learn to ride a bicycle? By reading the manual, watching others ride, or listening to instruction about keeping your balance? No. You'll never learn to ride a bike until you get on it and try—over and over and over. How do people learn to play the piano? By listening to the teacher play or learning to read sheet music? No. The only way to learn to play the piano is to practice those scales over and over again.

James likened the one who only hears God's Word but does not do it to "a man observing his natural face in a mirror; for he observes himself, goes away, and immediately forgets what kind of man he was." His message is all too clear. A mirror doesn't lie; it tells the truth. The Bible is like a mirror. When we look into it, we see ourselves as we really are in God's eyes, not who we say we are or who others might think we are.

Have you looked at yourself in the mirror of the Bible lately? Oh, I don't mean a passing glance. Stand there before it. Look at yourself in the mirror of Psalm 51 or Psalm 139. Take a good look. See yourself in these words: "Search me, O God, and know my heart; try me, and know my anxieties; and see if there is any wicked way in me, and lead me in the way everlasting" (Psalm 139:23–24). James talked about a man who "looks into the perfect law of liberty and continues in it, and is not a forgetful hearer but a doer of the work." James spoke of one who—every day—opens the Word and looks intently into it. As a result, this person stays on the Lord's course and is "blessed in what he does."

But God's blessings are just beginning when we hear biblical truth. Greater blessing comes with doing it, putting its truth into practice. We are not blessed in our stewardship and tithing, for instance, by studying what the Bible teaches, but in doing it.

James challenged us to "receive with meekness the implanted word, which is able to save your souls" (James 1:21). It's quite possible that James had Jesus' parable of the sower in mind when he penned these words. Jesus had compared His Word to seed and our hearts to soil. Some of the soil was fertile and received the seed. When we humbly receive God's Word in our hearts, it has a supernatural way of leading us to "be doers of the word and not hearers only." True faith involves not just knowing Christ, but also sowing consistency between what we read and hear *and* our conversation and our conduct.

JUST DO IT! It is vitally important to know God's Word, but it is even more important to obey it, to do it! Personally, I enjoy eating out. But I don't get satisfaction or nourishment if I just stare at the menu. Why should we think the Christian life is any different? Can we please Christ by staring at His menu? Satisfaction comes when the main course is served and we eat it. As the prophet said, "Your words were found, and I ate them, and Your word was to me the joy and rejoicing of my heart" (Jeremiah 15:16).

14   TRUE FAITH INVOLVES SHOWING CHARACTER

If anyone among you thinks he is religious, and does not bridle his tongue but deceives his own heart, this one's religion is useless. Pure and undefiled religion before God and the Father is this: to visit orphans and widows in their trouble, and to keep oneself unspotted from the world.

—JAMES 1:26–27

An inordinate amount of counterfeit Christianity seems to be cropping up. James was striking at this when he said, "If anyone among you thinks he is religious." Many people do, indeed, consider themselves religious. However, many approach religion like some kind of ecclesiastical cafeteria line. Some think they can go through the Bible picking and choosing commands they want to obey and leaving others for someone else. There are those who come across "Do not steal" and put it on their tray while passing up others like "Do not commit adultery." And, in the words of James, they still consider themselves religious, but their Christian faith is a sham.

As we've seen, credibility in the Christian life involves

knowing Christ and sowing consistency. It also involves showing character. And genuine Christian character is evident in three ways: by our conversation, our concern, and our conduct.

THE EVIDENCE OF OUR CONVERSATION

Our Christian character is shown in the way we converse. James said that those who consider themselves religious but don't "bridle [their] tongue" are deceiving themselves, and their religion is "useless" (James 1:26). In short, it's just an empty show.

The word we translate *deceive* can also mean "cheat." People who cannot control what comes out of their mouth—whether it is vile speech or gossip or slander or lies or whatever—are cheating themselves in the process. We have all known people like this and seen how they are actually deceiving themselves about their spiritual health.

When James said this type of conversation results in being "useless," he picked a word that literally means "without achieving its intended result or goal." A futile, fruitless religion is of no value to anyone.

Our character is often revealed in our conversation before anyone has a chance to observe our conduct. In James's words, it is therefore wise to "bridle [our] tongue."

THE EVIDENCE OF OUR CONCERN

True faith is demonstrated by our character, and our character is evident in what concerns us as well as by what we talk about. James continued: "Pure and undefiled religion before

God and the Father is this: to visit orphans and widows in their trouble."

Did James mean that proof of a pure religion is occasionally paying some of these folks a friendly visit? Not at all. James chose two of the most recognizably needy groups of people: orphans and widows. Remember, in the first century there were no life insurance policies or Social Security benefits, no orphanages or retirement homes. If the breadwinner died, orphaned children became victims of the street, often abused and traded by slave owners. Widows had no social standing, and some turned to immorality to provide for themselves. As Christians, we are to show mercy and kindness to people in such great need, especially to those who can never reciprocate.

But don't misunderstand. James wasn't suggesting we can be saved by good works. Salvation never results *from* good works, but it always results *in* good works.

James's command to visit those in need is a call to "look in on, to inspect." The Greek word literally means "to care for" these individuals. The word means much more than paying a simple visit to these people. After all, a true sign of Christian character is a genuine concern for anyone in need.

THE EVIDENCE OF OUR CONDUCT

James completed this initial chapter with an admonition to us to keep "unspotted from the world." The world system swirling around us has its own way of polluting many who are called by His name.

My wife often shops in a clearance center of a well-known national department store that is located not far from our home. Everything is marked down in price. She delights in telling me how much money she saves by shopping there so often. On an occasion there was a huge table with all sorts of odds and ends, shirts and shorts, sweaters and sneakers and the like piled upon it. A sign on the table read something to the effect, "Slightly soiled . . . Greatly reduced in price." How those words should penetrate your heart when you think of them—"Slightly soiled . . . greatly reduced in price." How many Christians have had those words written across their lives because of their inconsistent and ungodly conduct? Christians who allow their lives to become spotted and stained by sin lose much of the value of their Christian witness.

When James challenged us to keep "unspotted from the world," it was not a call to some kind of monkish isolationism. James was talking about *insulation*, not isolation. After all, Jesus Himself called us to be *in* the world but not *of* the world (John 17:14–17). As always, He is our example. And Jesus did not die wearing a starched white shirt with a nice tie, on a golden cross, on a mahogany communion table, or in an air-conditioned church with a high steeple and lots of stained glass. Jesus died out there among people who were sweating and cursing and gambling. And that is where He has told us to take His glorious good news, the gospel.

And so that our character shines brightly and credibly, we insulate ourselves from the world's influence by first knowing

Christ, then by sowing consistency in our lives, and, finally, by showing godly character in our conversation, our concerns, and our conduct.

As we, the church, seek to win new generations to Christ, one of the greatest issues we face is a credibility crisis of our own making. Are we credible witnesses for what we say we believe? The world is watching and waiting to see.

JUST DO IT! Our Lord ended the greatest sermon ever preached—the Sermon on the Mount—by telling the story of two different men who took the same architectural plans and built identical houses. When construction was complete, the houses looked alike . . . until the storm came. The winds blew with galelike force, the rain pelted the houses, and one fell flat while the other stood firm. Jesus explained that the house that fell flat had been built on shifting sand, and the one that still stood had been built on a foundation of solid rock. Jesus then revealed that the wise builder represented those who hear the Word of God and put it into practice, who *do* it (Matthew 7:24). In the words of James, "Be doers of the word, and not hearers only" (1:22). Just do it!

My brethren, do not hold the faith of our Lord Jesus Christ, the Lord of glory, with partiality. For if there should come into your assembly a man with gold rings, in fine apparel, and there should also come in a poor man in filthy clothes, and you pay attention to the one wearing the fine clothes and say to him, "You sit here in a good place," and say to the poor man, "You stand there," or, "Sit here at my footstool," have you not shown partiality among yourselves, and become judges with evil thoughts? Listen, my beloved brethren: Has God not chosen the poor of this world to be rich in faith and heirs of the kingdom which He promised to those who love Him? But you have dishonored the poor man. Do not the rich oppress you and drag you into the courts? Do they not blaspheme that noble name by which you are called? If you really fulfill the royal law according to the Scripture, "You shall love your neighbor as yourself," you do well; but if you show partiality, you commit sin, and are convicted by the law as transgressors.

—JAMES 2:1–9

*D*iscrimination was a problem in James's day, and discrimination lies at the root of many of the world's problems today despite some progress on certain fronts. In

South Africa, for instance, tremendous change has swept that nation. Racial equality now exists in that land of apartheid and strife. And it is hard to believe that here in America we are only two generations removed from racial segregation that at one time demanded separate schools, water fountains, and bathrooms. Yet tension still runs high in our land—and around the world—as discrimination continues to impact too many people.

Radical discrimination is obvious in the rapidly expanding Islamic terrorism that threatens death to the "infidels," those who hold religious beliefs different from theirs. As this global threat ravages the Middle East and enters pockets of the Western world, the brutal and senseless deaths of Jews, Christians, and even moderate Muslims result.

Ironically, the victim of some of the most intense public discrimination in America is conservative Christianity. As a result of anti-Christian bigotry, nativity scenes have been removed from town squares, Christmas carols are banned in most public schools, and the Ten Commandments are removed from county buildings. In more and more places, abortion information can be obtained without parental consent, and the Gideons are restricted from distributing Bibles the way they've done for decades. Secularists have taken advantage of the fact that many Christians simply turn the other cheek rather than fight for their rights like our Jewish friends do through their Anti-Defamation League or our liberal friends with their American Civil Liberties Union.

James called upon the church to address the issue of

discrimination. One would hope that after two thousand years of church history these words of James 2:1–7 would be archaic and irrelevant. Unfortunately, they are as applicable today and therefore as necessary as ever.

Even as it's the victim of discrimination, the church of the Lord Jesus ought to be one place where discrimination is not tolerated. Unfortunately that isn't so. Consider that the majority of most congregations look the same, dress the same, talk the same, and come from the same economic and social levels. Yet sermons on discrimination are the far exception rather than the rule.

Maybe one reason for the church's silence is that discrimination can be very subtle today. Some people still discriminate on the basis of race. Others discriminate based on income and have little to do with those not at their own economic level. Some have little respect for others unless they share the same social standing or they are of the same sex.

Discrimination can work both ways. Some Christians with money discriminate against those without it, and some without money discriminate against the wealthier with responses of jealousy, envy, and suspicion. I have known whites who discriminate against blacks and some blacks who discriminate against whites. The same could be said for Jews and Gentiles, for heterosexuals and homosexuals, and for men and women in the workplace.

Although I didn't realize it at the time, I witnessed an object lesson about discrimination when, as a child, I saw the circus at the old Will Rogers Coliseum in Fort Worth. I was particularly intrigued by a certain clown act. One clown was a giant of a man standing almost eight feet tall (of course, I later found out that his pants covered the stilts he was walking around on), and his partner was a little person barely three feet tall. These two characters carried on in such a fashion that the entire audience was soon laughing uproariously. The tall man got the best of the short man until the very final moments of their act. At that point, the little person sneaked up behind him and knocked the stilts out from under him, revealing the fact that he, too, was a little person.

I share this story to make an important point. The vile sin of discrimination stands on two false legs that need to be knocked out from under it. One of those legs is prejudice; the other is presumption. The truth James set forth two millennia ago can help knock those false legs out from under this enemy of the church today.

JUST DO IT! According to the Great Commandment, referred to as the "royal law" in James 2:8, we are to "love [our] neighbor as [ourselves]." However, on the evening before the crucifixion, Jesus gave us what He called a "new commandment": He called us to "love one another; as I have loved you . . . love one another" (John 13:34). Until Jesus issued that command, we were to love on the self-love level of the old commandment. But obedience to this new commandment means loving the people around us in the same way Jesus loves us: selflessly and sacrificially. Ask God to help you begin to see others around you through His eyes today and to love them with His love.

16   *The* FALSE LEG *of* PREJUDICE

My brethren, do not hold the faith of our Lord Jesus Christ, the Lord of glory, with partiality. For if there should come into your assembly a man with gold rings, in fine apparel, and there should also come in a poor man in filthy clothes, and you pay attention to the one wearing the fine clothes and say to him, "You sit here in a good place," and say to the poor man, "You stand there," or, "Sit here at my footstool," have you not shown partiality among yourselves, and become judges with evil thoughts? Listen, my beloved brethren: Has God not chosen the poor of this world to be rich in faith and heirs of the kingdom which He promised to those who love Him? But you have dishonored the poor man. Do not the rich oppress you and drag you into the courts? Do they not blaspheme that noble name by which you are called?

—JAMES 2:1–7

AN EXPLANATION

Prejudice is a bias built upon a fixed idea. It is often an opinion arrived at without taking time to evaluate something fairly. Many wars and even world conflicts have been the direct result of prejudicial thinking. Prejudice is one of the false legs upon which discrimination stands.

James took a firm stand against prejudice, against coming to a conclusion based only on an external appearance. James warned, "Don't do that. Don't show partiality or favoritism based on what you see on the outside."

James's warning here was not to those in the political or social arena; he was specifically addressing the church. Our Lord Jesus never looked at outward appearances but instead on the heart. Jesus is still not impressed by how many goods we have accumulated, whom we know, or how high we have climbed up the social ladder. Jesus had as much respect for the poor unnamed widow offering her two pennies as He did for wealthy Joseph of Arimathea. And Jesus was known for His compassion.

But the people James was addressing apparently flattered the rich in hopes of getting something from them. So James said, "Stop this prejudicial behavior. Don't show favoritism." We are never more like Jesus than when we look to the heart of others instead of on their outward appearance. Prejudice shouldn't have a leg to stand on in the Christian faith.

AN ILLUSTRATION

James illustrated this truth, saying, "If there should come into your assembly a man with gold rings, in fine apparel, and there should also come in a poor man in filthy clothes, and you pay attention to the one wearing the fine clothes and say to him, 'You sit here in a good place,' and say to the poor man, 'You stand there,' or, 'Sit here at my footstool,' have you not shown partiality among yourselves, and become judges with evil thoughts?" (2:2–4).

Picture this. A worship service is about to start. In walk two men. One is wearing an expensive designer suit, a gold watch, and a diamond ring. The other's clothes don't fit properly and most likely came from a clothing ministry. An usher guides the first man to the best seat in the house and instructs the latter to go stand in the corner, out of the way. The problem is not that the usher found a good seat for the wealthy man; the problem is that the usher showed no respect for the poorer man. But realize, too, that poverty does not make a person special in God's eyes.

When I was pastoring in Fort Lauderdale, God blessed me through two different men. One was extremely wealthy. For years he had been a quiet backbone of the church. He generally sat at the rear of the sanctuary, and he never pushed himself into leadership. But he did more anonymously to help struggling people than anyone I have ever known. The other man lived in an institutional center not far from the church. His pants were always about two sizes too big. The cuffs were rolled halfway up his calves, revealing sockless feet and worn tennis shoes. His shirt was buttoned in the wrong holes more often than not. And there he sat in the front row every Sunday. Only heaven knows how many times I looked at his face and breathed a prayer of thanksgiving to God for this reminder of how welcome the outcasts of society should be in God's house.

Again, we must be careful not to confuse the issue here. There is nothing wrong with wealth. It is "the love of money," not money itself, that is the root of evil (1 Timothy 6:10). It is also wrong to have the mind-set that if we have money, we are better than someone who does not. On the contrary, some who have little money love it more than those who have lots of it. Put differently, it is not sinful to be rich, and it is not spiritual to be poor. But it is always wrong to show partiality based solely on outward appearances. Discrimination stands on a shaky leg of prejudice, and James exposed it here.

AN ACCUSATION

James's accusation is stinging: "You have dishonored the poor man" and taken away his dignity. We should guard against dishonoring anyone, especially those whose dignity is about all that they have. Let us keep in mind that Jesus said, "Inasmuch as you did it to one of the least of these My brethren, you did it to Me" (Matthew 25:40). To paraphrase James, "Don't deny their dignity; don't steal their honor."

James also made this point: "Has God not chosen the poor of this world to be rich in faith and heirs of the kingdom which He promised to those who love Him?" Have you noticed that the poor often seem to grasp the gospel in greater numbers than the rich and more privileged do? In general, those who have materially less are more aware of their powerlessness, so it is easier for some of them to recognize their need for salvation. Often the rich and powerful, however, see no reason to have Christ in their lives. Frequently, the greatest barrier to reaching the wealthy with the gospel is their pride, while the greatest barrier to reaching the poor can be their self-pity and bitterness.

As if giving rich people places of honor based solely on outward appearance weren't bad enough, the people James addressed were at the same time pushing back into a corner the very people among whom Jesus spent His entire ministry. Our Lord never showed such partiality. When He went to Jerusalem, He spent time with an invalid at the Pool of Bethesda as well as with Nicodemus, a ruler of the Jews. When Jesus journeyed through Jericho, He called out to rich Zacchaeus who was perched in a tree, and He healed blind Bartimaeus who was begging by the roadside.

Early believers knew this about Jesus, and one of the reasons the early church grew so rapidly was that prejudice was laid aside. Although the Jews and Samaritans despised each other passionately, Jesus made a place for Nicodemus, a ruler of the Jews, as well as the woman at the well of Sychar who was the former town prostitute. As the early church grew, it made room for Onesimus, the former slave, at the same table as Philemon, the wealthy landowner and his former master. Wealthy Barnabas gave a piece of real estate to the missionary church at Antioch, and alongside him was a place for a blind beggar rattling a tin cup asking for alms. The gospel gives everyone, everywhere a place of dignity at Christ's table.

Yes, the vile sin of discrimination stands on two false legs. One of these is prejudice, which has no place in the heart of a true believer. The other leg, as we shall see next, is presumption.

JUST DO IT! The ancient prophet Habakkuk climbed up in his watchtower in order to "watch to see what [God] will say to me" (Habakkuk 2:1). I sometimes fear that too much of our Christian experience is taken up with our saying something to God or each other; we spend too little time getting alone to listen to God. He definitely has something to say to us about discrimination—and He is not whispering. Ask Him to help you view people around you today through His eyes. You just might see a few folks differently than you have in the past.

17   *The* FALSE LEG *of* PRESUMPTION

If you really fulfill the royal law according to the Scripture, "You shall love your neighbor as yourself," you do well; but if you show partiality, you commit sin, and are convicted by the law as transgressors. For whoever shall keep the whole law, and yet stumble in one point, he is guilty of all. For He who said, "Do not commit adultery," also said, "Do not murder." Now if you do not commit adultery, but you do murder, you have become a transgressor of the law. So speak and so do as those who will be judged by the law of liberty. For judgment is without mercy to the one who has shown no mercy. Mercy triumphs over judgment.

—JAMES 2:8–13

*P*eople who discriminate are presumptuous. They presume that discrimination is not sin, is not significant, and is not serious. But like the stilts a clown stands on, these false presumptions are easily knocked down.

PRESUMPTION #1: DISCRIMINATION IS NOT SIN

Some people are so settled in a lifestyle of discrimination that they seldom, if ever, give it any serious thought. How many times have we heard, "Well, I am from such and such a state, and that's just the way it is down there." These people falsely presume that God is simply smiling and saying, "Oh yes, I know how it is where you grew up." But in God's eyes that explanation has zero merit; it is no excuse. Discrimination is sin. To presume otherwise is to make a false presumption.

James was very straightforward about that fact: "If you show partiality, you commit sin, and are convicted by the law as transgressors." The Bible calls discrimination a sin. God is as serious about the sin of partiality and prejudice as He the sin of perversion and promiscuity. So if we are guilty of discrimination, we should deal with it like we deal with every other sin: confess it and forsake it.

James commanded us to abide by Jesus' command: "Love the Lord your God with all your heart, with all your soul, and with all your mind. . . . Love your neighbor as yourself" (Matthew 22:37–39). This great commandment is called the royal law not only because it is given to us by the King of kings, but also because it is the law that governs citizens of His kingdom.

But followers of Jesus are saved by God's grace (Ephesians 2:8). So what is our relationship to the law? To begin, remember that God did not give us the law to save us. No one has ever earned salvation by keeping the law, and no one ever will. The law is our tutor, our teacher, to show us how futile it is to think we could get to heaven through our good works, through obedience to the law. But does this mean that since Christ has come, we are no longer subject to the law and its demands? On this side of the cross, we are under the royal law of love. Jesus never came to do away with the law, and He made this very clear in His Sermon on the Mount. Jesus took the law and made it a matter of the heart. He made it a matter of love, which was the original intent of the Lawgiver in the first place. This is why Paul wrote, "Stand fast therefore in the liberty by which Christ has made us free, and do not be entangled again with a yoke of bondage" (Galatians 5:1), meaning the law.

Again, living on this side of the cross, we are not governed by external laws and rules, but by the royal law of love. Those who love God with their entire being and who love the people around them will certainly have no problem living within the parameters of the moral code of the Mosaic law. And, according to this royal law, discrimination is a sin, and those who practice it do not have a leg to stand on.

PRESUMPTION #2: DISCRIMINATION IS NOT SIGNIFICANT

Those who discriminate against others are so blind to their own sin that if they even acknowledge that they discriminate against others, they don't think of it as being that significant. "After all, it's not as if we committed murder or adultery!" James penned this epistle to people—then, and now—who live with the erroneous idea that sins of disrespect, favoritism, partiality, and discrimination are not that significant. James made it crystal clear what God thinks of this.

James wrote, "For whoever shall keep the whole law, and yet stumble in one point, he is guilty of all." Let those words

sink in. Without the mercy of God and the grace of the Lord Jesus Christ, one sin—no matter how small it may seem—is enough to condemn a person. Jesus died for the sin of discrimination as much as for any other sin. Only we rank sins' severity.

This discussion should put to rest forever the idea that any of us can get to heaven on the basis of good works, a solid reputation, or our relative morality. Some seem to think they can stand before the Judge of the universe and appeal to Him on the basis of the sins they have *not* committed. That will go about as far as standing before a municipal judge with a speeding ticket pleading for leniency on the basis of the fact you have never robbed a bank or committed murder.

To be a lawbreaker, one does not have to break all the laws—only one. But to be a law abider, one must keep all the laws. We break the royal law of love when we discriminate against others. Discrimination is a sin, and it is significant. Don't presume otherwise.

PRESUMPTION #3: DISCRIMINATION IS NOT SERIOUS

Some people are presumptuous enough to think that although discrimination may well be a sin, it isn't that serious. But James continued: "So speak and so do as those who will be judged by the law of liberty. For judgment is without mercy to the one who has shown no mercy. Mercy triumphs over judgment." Because of the judgment that awaits each of us, it is presumptuous to conclude that discrimination is not that serious. We should speak and act as those who will one day be judged by our words and works.

James drove home the point that law and liberty actually come together in beautiful harmony. In fact, he called it "the law of liberty." The way to find true freedom is to live within the boundaries God has set for us. After all, Jesus said it is the truth that ultimately sets us free (John 8:31–32).

Those who continue to live outside the parameters God has set for us aren't really free. They cover one lie with another, wondering if they will be found out and unknowingly become slaves to their own sin. Only a fool would argue that sin is not serious.

James concluded his discourse on discrimination by saying, "Mercy triumphs over judgment." The word *triumph* literally means "to have no fear of something." Those who show mercy to others have no fear of judgment. The one who extends mercy is not afraid of the coming day when he will stand before the great Judge who knows the hearts of all men and women. Yes, mercy triumphs over judgment.

If we are unmerciful—if we are guilty of the sin of discrimination—what can we do? We can stop blaming that sin on our background or upbringing. Just because our parents might have been adulterers or murderers doesn't mean we have to be also. And just because we grew up in a culture of discrimination doesn't mean we should continue in it. We must deal with discrimination by seeing it as God sees it: discrimination is sin. Thus, we deal with discrimination the same way we deal with every other sin we commit. We

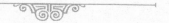

admit it. We confess it. We forsake it. And God forgives it. And mercy triumphs over judgment!

JUST DO IT! Some of us are trying to navigate through life by standing on the false legs of prejudice and presumption. Thank God that Jesus is no respecter of persons. He never shows favoritism. He reaches out to each of us—to you and me—at the very point of our need. Jesus knows you—including all those hidden thoughts of your heart. And He loves you—deeply. He loves you so much that He took upon Himself all your sin, suffered, and died your death so you could live forgiven of your sin and in relationship with Him. Admit. Confess. Forsake. Mercy still triumphs over judgment.

18 *The* ETHICAL EFFECT

What does it profit, my brethren, if someone says he has faith but does not have works? Can faith save him? If a brother or sister is naked and destitute of daily food, and one of you says to them, "Depart in peace, be warmed and filled," but you do not give them the things which are needed for the body, what does it profit? Thus also faith by itself, if it does not have works, is dead. But someone will say, "You have faith, and I have works." Show me your faith without your works, and I will show you my faith by my works. You believe that there is one God. You do well. Even the demons believe—and tremble! But do you want to know, O foolish man, that faith without works is dead? Was not Abraham our father justified by works when he offered Isaac his son on the altar? Do you see that faith was working together with his works, and by works faith was made perfect? And the Scripture was fulfilled which says, "Abraham believed God, and it was accounted to him for righteousness." And he was called the friend of God. You see then that a man is justified by works, and not by faith only. Likewise, was not Rahab the harlot also justified by works when she received the messengers and sent them out another way? For as the body without the spirit is dead, so faith without works is dead also.

—JAMES 2:14–26

*W*e live in a day when the news reports on an "effect" of some kind or another. For example, there is the "greenhouse effect," a type of global warming that may impact our climate and overall environment in the future. We hear in sociopolitical discussions about the "domino effect." In the last decade of the twentieth century, like dominos, one Eastern European nation after another broke free of Soviet oppression.

The church today faces its own effect, what could be called the "ethical effect," or, as James might have put it, "a faith without fruit." As the world watches, too many Christians profess one thing but practice another, faking their faith and forfeiting any fruit. In the not-too-distant past, the church was the most respected and influential institution in virtually every American community. Now, in large part because of the ethical effect, the church has little influence in our culture. While we are still vocal about proclaiming our faith, much of the world shouts back at us with the question of James 2:14, 16—"What good is all this talk about faith?"

In so many places and in so many ways, the church is losing its voice as our culture also suffers from this ethical effect. An integrity crisis is running rampant in every aspect of our society. Time and space keep us from illustrating here how the ethical effect has touched government, politics, business, law, medicine, sports, and, unfortunately, religion. The ethical effect has brought down high-profile individuals in every professional field. Our world needs people whose lives match their lips, whose walk matches their talk.

As we journey with James through this section of verses, we now enter a room where a contentious debate has flared up from time to time over the past twenty centuries. James 2:14–26 is like a boxing ring where the church has pitted Paul, with his emphasis on faith, against James, with his emphasis on works, as if it were the biggest prize fight ever held. I can hear the announcer now: "In this corner, wearing the grace trunks, is the apostle Paul. His claim is 'By grace you have been saved through faith, and that not of yourselves' (Ephesians 2:8). And in the other corner, wearing the works trunks, is James. He maintains that faith without works is dead . . . DOA . . . dead on arrival."

Make no mistake about it—the Bible plainly teaches that our eternal salvation rests entirely on God's grace and is appropriated through our faith in the finished work of Christ. Salvation is the free gift of God to everyone who will receive it. The Bible also says that true, saving faith will always result in good works. After all, how could the living Christ take up residency in your life, be alive *in you*, and not make any difference in the way you think and act?

This entire debate hinges on the failure of some to make a distinction between the *requirement* for true salvation and the *result* of true salvation. Good works are never a requirement for salvation, but they are certainly the result. People who have passed from death to life and from darkness to light, who have had their sins forgiven, and who have become new creations in Christ can't help but see the world differently and respond accordingly.

In the faith-versus-works debate, people tend to gravitate toward the extremes. Some overemphasize the faith aspect while completely neglecting the fact that it should result in good works. According to this "faith, *not* works" school of thought, people can pray a simple "sinner's prayer," have no change of lifestyle, develop no desire to pray, never open a Bible, exhibit zero desire for spiritual things, yet still be saved because they "believed." I call this an easy believism.

Other believers argue for "faith *or* works." If you say you have faith, that's fine with them. Or if you do good works around the community, that's also fine. This universalist mentality trusts that ultimately everyone will arrive at some type of utopian existence.

There are also individuals who come to these verses and start arguing for "faith *and* works." This mind-set overemphasizes works and de-emphasizes faith. These adherents of a works salvation somehow think there's a way to earn our way into eternal life.

It's at this point of our journey that James revealed to us the code we need to understand the relationship of faith and works. Here it is—and underline it in red: salvation is not about faith *and* works; it is about a faith *that* works! If you can grasp this simple sentence, you will understand the heart of the entire issue. The church today desperately needs to rediscover a faith *that* works—a faith that bears fruit. After all, a faith that has no fruit is a false faith—a futile faith—and, worse, a fatal faith.

JUST DO IT!

Paul and James have been in the ring sparring about faith versus works. But when the final bell rings, they are both still standing. In fact, they grab each other's arms in victory and raise them high. They both win! How? Because they are both saying the same thing (Ephesians 2:10; James 1:18). They complement, not contradict, each other. Paul emphasized faith because he wrote primarily to the Judaizers, people of the Jewish faith who had proclaimed to the early church the false teaching that new Christ-followers had to add works to faith. That inaccurate teaching is why Paul strongly emphasized faith. In contrast, James wrote to people who went to the other extreme, who understood faith as being the key to salvation but didn't care about the fruit of that faith. That's why James emphasized that works are a result of true salvation, not a requirement for salvation. So Paul and James leave the ring arm in arm: faith *and* works. And that's the way it should be, because salvation is not about faith *or* works, but about a faith *that* works.

19   A Faith Without Fruit Is *a* False Faith

What does it profit, my brethren, if someone says he has faith but does not have works? Can faith save him? If a brother or sister is naked and destitute of daily food, and one of you says to them, "Depart in peace, be warmed and filled," but you do not give them the things which are needed for the body, what does it profit? Thus also faith by itself, if it does not have works, is dead.

— JAMES 2:14–17

AN EXPLANATION

*J*ames wasted no time getting to the heart of the issue in this passage. He began with a question: "What does it profit—what good is it—if someone claims to have faith but doesn't back up that claim with actions?" To put it bluntly, a faith without any accompanying fruit is a false faith. Earlier, on a Galilean hillside, our Lord had said the very same thing in a different way: "By their fruits you will know them" (Matthew 7:20).

Observe carefully what James was actually saying—and note what he did not say as well. James was not referring to a man who has faith, but to someone who "says he has faith."

James was addressing a false claim to faith, not the nature of genuine faith. The mere claim that one is a believer does not make him such. Many people today say they are people of faith, but they have never placed their faith in Christ alone and experienced what Jesus called "the new birth." In fact, Jesus framed it rather bluntly: "Not everyone who says to Me, 'Lord, Lord,' shall enter the kingdom of heaven" (Matthew 7:21).

Much of the unnecessary confusion in the faith-works debate stems from the translation of James's second question in James 2:14. Both the King James Version and the New King James Version ask, "Can faith save him?" The Greek text has an article in front of the word *faith*, indicating that this faith is the same faith just mentioned in the first question of verse 14—that is, a false faith. Properly translated, the question reads, "Can such a faith, can *that* kind of a faith, save him?" James was certainly *not* saying that faith cannot save a person, but that a faith characterized only by intellectual assent but exhibits no fruit is, in the final analysis, a false faith.

Every Sunday multiplied thousands of people say they have faith. But James asked, "What does it profit, my brethren, if someone says he has faith but does not have works? Can [that kind of] faith save him?" The answer is no.

AN ILLUSTRATION

Having described a false faith, James proceeded to illustrate it. He painted the picture of someone in need of food and clothing, the basic necessities of life. This person is not a professional con artist or streetwise person with a slothful lifestyle, but someone with a legitimate and immediate need. A person who claims to have faith goes to him, puts his hand on his shoulder, pats him on the back, and says, "Have a good day. Be careful out there and try to stay warm. I hope you find something to eat. Bless you."

Then came the rhetorical question: "What good does that response do for the hungry and cold man?" James was shining the spotlight on those of us who seem to prefer words over works, who know how to talk a good faith game yet have no impact on the world around us because our faith does not produce fruit.

AN APPLICATION

A glib "Good luck" to a person who is hungry does not relieve his immediate need. Thus, James continued, "Faith, by itself, if it does not have works, is dead." That is, faith without any fruit doesn't do you or anyone else any good. It is a false faith.

The only way to know if faith is genuine is by its fruit. Now, before any of us get too self-righteous, we should remember that God didn't put us on the judgment committee. In fact, Jesus warned, "Judge not, that you be not judged" (Matthew 7:1). However, in that same sermon Jesus later said, "By their fruits you will know (recognize) them" (v. 20). We are never to stand in judgment of others, but we are expected to have the spiritual sensitivity necessary to be fruit inspectors.

Recently, I was called to jury duty. Judges and lawyers are quick to tell you that in a trial there is no place for hearsay. Only hard, cold facts qualify as indisputable evidence, a truth

that reminds me of a question we all should ask ourselves: "If you were arrested for being a Christian, would there be enough evidence to convict you?" More specifically, would anyone be able to take the stand on your behalf to say—in Jesus' words— "I was hungry and you gave Me food; I was thirsty and you gave Me drink; I was a stranger and you took Me in; I was naked and you clothed Me; I was sick and you visited Me; I was in prison and you came to Me" (Matthew 25:35–36)?

One more note about faith and works. Among the legacy of the Reformers is their often-repeated affirmation, "It is faith alone that saves, but faith that saves is never alone." In James's words, "Faith by itself, if it does not have works, is dead." Remember, James was not talking about faith *and* works but about a faith *that* works.

JUST DO IT! In the ancient world, someone finding a person who appeared to be dead would hold a mirror under that person's nose. If the mirror got cloudy, it indicated that life was in the body even though the person was barely breathing. If the mirror stayed clear after a brief while, it was evident that the person was dead. In this section of his letter, James took the mirror of God's Word and held it under our noses. Is our faith breathing? A faith without works is dead. A faith without fruit is a false faith.

20   A FAITH WITHOUT FRUIT IS *a* FUTILE FAITH

Someone will say, "You have faith, and I have works." Show me your faith without your works, and I will show you my faith by my works. You believe that there is one God. You do well. Even the demons believe—and tremble!

—JAMES 2:18–19

AN EXPLANATION

A faith that does not produce fruit is not only false; it is also futile.

In a creative dialogue with an imaginary person, James continued addressing the matter of those who profess a good game but whose faith, in the end, is merely talk.

James engaged his readers with this challenge: "Show me your faith without your works, and I will show you my faith by my works." This two-letter, one-syllable word *by* translates a Greek preposition that is best understood as "out of." James was saying that our works emerge "out of" our true faith in Christ. Paul actually echoed this very point, saying, "By grace you have been saved through faith, and that not of yourselves; it is the gift of God, not of works, lest anyone should boast.

For we are His workmanship, created in Christ Jesus for good works" (Ephesians 2:8–10). The apostle left no doubt that faith alone is the channel of God's saving grace. Then, like James, Paul added a word about the proof of faith being our good works: we are "created in Christ Jesus for good works." Both Paul and James talked about a faith *that* works. When we examine what each of them really said, we see that they arrived at the same point even though they came to it from different directions. Paul and James never contradicted each other; their teachings complemented each other.

When Paul spoke of works in his epistles, he was generally speaking of the works of the law, like observing the Sabbath and the like. However, when James spoke of works, he was referring to the fruit of genuine faith, to obedience issuing out of love. A clearer understanding of what each man is saying comes when we remember their audiences. If Paul were alive today, he would be addressing those who think they can be saved by keeping the law through their own human effort. That's why Paul's emphasis fell solidly on the side of grace. If James were around today, his argument would be directed to those who adhere to a cheap faith that tends to say, "I am saved and under grace, so I don't have to even think about the law. I can live any way I desire."

AN ILLUSTRATION

James chose to illustrate a futile faith with demons, of all things. James said, "You believe there is one God. You do well. Even the demons believe—and tremble!" It may surprise

some to discover that demons have faith. They are surely not atheists, or even agnostics. They believe in the one true God. As the possessed man in the synagogue in Capernaum asked, "What have we to do with You, Jesus of Nazareth? Did You come to destroy us? I know who You are—the Holy One of God!" (Mark 1:24). During Jesus' healing ministry in Galilee, the "unclean spirits, whenever they saw Him, fell down before Him and cried out, saying, 'You are the Son of God'" (Mark 3:11). In his gospel, Luke recorded that "demons also came out of many, crying out and saying, 'You are the Christ, the Son of God!'" (Luke 4:41).

Yes, even the Devil and his demons believe. They recognize the holiness of God and the deity of Christ, but they do not possess saving faith. Their faith is an intellectual assent that goes no further than mere head knowledge of who Jesus really is. Yet that head knowledge is enough to make the demons tremble in terror at the coming judgment.

It is strange to realize that many professing believers today are farther from God than the demons. Many professing believers almost robotically go through the motions of a lifeless faith with no real fear of God.

AN APPLICATION

Even before our spiritual birth that came with trusting in Christ alone for our salvation, most of us believed the facts of Christ's story. Few of us were bona fide atheists or agnostics. But the gospel did not alter our lives in any way. Many today believe that Jesus died on a cross in much the same way

that we believe George Washington was the first president of the United States. They acknowledge that He existed as a real person; they simply do not trust their lives and eternal destiny to Him. The tragedy is that their false and futile faith does not really bother these people. Yet without true saving faith—and that comes only by God's grace and through our faith, through our trust in Christ alone rather than any effort on our part—our faith is false and futile.

JUST DO IT! The prophet Isaiah preached the gospel well: "All we like sheep have gone astray; we have turned, every one, to his own way; and the Lord has laid on Him the iniquity of us all" (Isaiah 53:6). Every sin you ever committed—every bad thing you have done and every good thing you chose not to do—Christ took in His own body and suffered the punishment you deserved. He took on your sin—so that you can take on His righteousness. He died your death—so you can live His life. He took on Himself the very wrath of God that you deserved so you could receive the very grace of God that none of us deserves. As Paul put it, "If you confess with your mouth the Lord Jesus and believe in your heart that God has raised [Christ] from the dead, you will be saved" (Romans 10:9). Stop trying. Start trusting.

21 A Faith Without Fruit Is *a* Fatal Faith

Do you want to know, O foolish man, that faith without works is dead? Was not Abraham our father justified by works when he offered Isaac his son on the altar? Do you see that faith was working together with his works, and by works faith was made perfect? And the Scripture was fulfilled which says, "Abraham believed God, and it was accounted to him for righteousness." And he was called the friend of God. You see then that a man is justified by works, and not by faith only. Likewise, was not Rahab the harlot also justified by works when she received the messengers and sent them out another way? For as the body without the spirit is dead, so faith without works is dead also.

—JAMES 2:20–26

AN EXPLANATION

A faith without works is not simply false and futile; worse, it is fatal. James bluntly called it "dead." No pulse. No vital signs. No heartbeat. Only a fatal silence. That so-called faith is DOA, dead on arrival.

James went so far as to call the person without faith "foolish," a word that describes someone who is an impostor. On other occasions in the New Testament, that word is translated "empty-handed" or "empty" (Mark 12:3; Luke 1:53). James's point is plain: people who only talk faith but don't walk with accompanied good works lead an empty life because their faith is not alive and working. Their faith is dead.

AN ILLUSTRATION

Like a skilled attorney who has stated his case, James now laid out his facts. He offered the court two witnesses: a revered patriarch and a reformed prostitute.

When Abraham took the stand, James asked, "Was not Abraham our father justified by works when he offered Isaac his son on the altar?" This question seems to directly contradict what Paul said of Abraham: "If Abraham was justified by works, he has something to boast about, but not before God. For what does the Scripture say? 'Abraham believed God, and it was accounted to him for righteousness'" (Romans 4:2–3). Actually, these two statements regarding this faithful patriarch complement rather than contradict each other.

Some have suggested that James was simply answering Paul's argument, but that's impossible. James may have written his epistle as early as AD 48, and Paul did not pen the Roman letter until at least AD 58. Paul was emphasizing that no one enters God's kingdom except by faith, and James agreed. James was not arguing that works are a requirement for salvation, but that works are the result of a true born-again experience.

James was arguing that "faith was working together with

his works, and by works faith was made perfect." The Greek behind *working together* gives us the English word *synergy*. When faith is joined by works in a believer's life, a new and synergistic dynamic results. Faith and works are not to exist separately; they work together.

Furthermore, by quoting Genesis 15:6—"[Abraham] believed in the Lord, and He accounted it to him for righteousness"—James was certainly not disagreeing with Paul, but adding that genuine faith is evidenced by fruit. Genesis 15 is the account of Abraham's salvation. Abraham was not saved by his good works or by keeping the Jewish law. Abraham was saved in the same way we are today: by faith. The only difference is that Abraham was looking forward to God's promise of redemption in the coming Messiah, and we are looking backward to the same event. To leave no doubt, Jesus also referred to Abraham's forward-looking faith: "Your father Abraham rejoiced to see My day, and he saw it and was glad" (John 8:56).

Abraham had a genuine faith that resulted in good works. He was put to the test thirty years later when God instructed him to take Isaac, his only son, and sacrifice him on Mt. Moriah. Abraham obeyed God completely, and the writer of Hebrews memorialized it for all time: "By faith Abraham, when he was tested, offered up Isaac . . . concluding that God was able to raise him up, even from the dead" (Hebrews 11:17, 19). Thus James rightly asked, "Was not Abraham our father justified by works when he offered Isaac his son on the altar?"

James went on to say that Abraham's faith was "accounted

to him for righteousness." In some translations we read *credited* for righteousness. In Greek this is an accountant's term meaning that we take a payment from someone but enter it into someone else's accounts received ledger. Like yours—like mine—Abraham's spiritual bank account was empty. We were all spiritually bankrupt. When Abraham trusted in God, God made a deposit in his account. Abraham didn't work for it; he couldn't earn it. That deposit of Jesus' righteousness was a gift in response to Abraham's faith. That same deposit was made in my account when, as a seventeen-year-old, I heard the gospel and placed my trust in the saving grace of Christ. Our righteousness is imputed to us, given to us by God Himself, deposited into our account on the basis of our faith in Jesus our Savior.

After presenting a faithful prophet as evidence that saving faith is revealed in works, James turned to a former prostitute: "Likewise, was not Rahab the harlot also justified by works when she received the messengers and sent them out another way?" Abraham had a reputation of morality, but Rahab was known for her immorality. As a Gentile, she was outside the Jewish covenant, not inside. She was rejected from society, not respected by it. Yet James introduced her with the word *likewise*: in the exact way Abraham found grace, so did Rahab. The two of them walked different paths, but they—like us— arrived at the point of salvation in the same way: by faith.

Rahab's life certainly wouldn't have led anyone to expect her to arrive at a saving faith. But before the spies went to Jericho in anticipation of the conquest of the promised land,

Rahab had heard how God had been with them, parting the Red Sea and enabling them to defeat the Amorite kings, and she put her faith in the God of Abraham, Isaac, and Jacob. Her hiding God's messengers and later hanging the scarlet thread of salvation out her window did not earn her salvation. These acts were the simple responses of one who was living by faith. As the writer of Hebrews confirmed, "By faith the harlot Rahab did not perish with those who did not believe, when she had received the spies with peace" (Hebrews 11:31).

In these two illustrations, a revered prophet and a reformed prostitute were both declared righteous on the basis of their faith, and theirs was a faith that worked. True faith always produces fruit. And that's why, in the great roll call of the faithful in Hebrews 11, each person is introduced with the phrase *By faith*—and that phrase is followed by a specific act of obedience. Our faith in God is not real unless it moves us to action.

AN APPLICATION

James concluded his discourse on faith and works by showing that faith and its fruit are as essential to each other as the body and the spirit are: "For as the body without the spirit is dead, so faith without works is dead also." Or, as James said bluntly, "Faith without works is dead."

It's possible to have no faith and no works. It's also possible to have works and no faith. But it's impossible to have true saving faith and no works. But biblical Christianity is not about faith *and* works either. Salvation begins with faith alone, but genuine Christianity is about a faith *that* works.

JUST DO IT! God deposited His own righteousness into your account: He credited it to you. Suppose you overextended yourself on your credit card and could not pay the full amount when the bill arrived. You open the envelope only to find out that someone else has paid off your debt in full and even deposited an amount from which you can draw in the future. This is what happens when God responds to your faith in Him by imputing His own righteousness to your salvation account. We all owed a debt for our sin that we could not pay. Jesus, who never sinned, went to the cross, took our sin in His own body, and—with His life—paid for us the debt He did not owe. That gift truly is amazing grace.

22   WORDS AS WELL AS WORKS

My brethren, let not many of you become teachers, knowing that we shall receive a stricter judgment. For we all stumble in many things. If anyone does not stumble in word, he is a perfect man, able also to bridle the whole body. Indeed, we put bits in horses' mouths that they may obey us, and we turn their whole body. Look also at ships: although they are so large and are driven by fierce winds, they are turned by a very small rudder wherever the pilot desires. Even so the tongue is a little member and boasts great things. See how great a forest a little fire kindles! And the tongue is a fire, a world of iniquity. The tongue is so set among our members that it defiles the whole body, and sets on fire the course of nature; and it is set on fire by hell. For every kind of beast and bird, of reptile and creature of the sea, is tamed and has been tamed by mankind. But no man can tame the tongue. It is an unruly evil, full of deadly poison. With it we bless our God and Father, and with it we curse men, who have been made in the similitude of God. Out of the same mouth proceed blessing and cursing. My brethren, these things ought not to be so. Does a spring send forth fresh water and bitter from the same opening? Can a fig tree, my brethren, bear olives, or a grapevine bear figs? Thus no spring yields both salt water and fresh.

—JAMES 3:1–12

For the past several years, talk radio has come to fill more and more of America's airwaves. We are a nation of talkers. We have something to say, and, it seems, most everyone wants to be heard. The disappearing print media still have their opinion pages, but talk shows have cornered the conviction market. There is no shortage of deep-rooted convictions blasting through the airwaves at any hour, day or night.

But words don't become public through our lips alone. Social media venues (Facebook, Twitter, e-mail, YouTube, Instagram, and the like) are making verbal communication a dying art. The vast majority of communication today takes place via a smartphone text or computer. (Who would have thought so much could be said with only 140 characters on Twitter?) And who can predict what tomorrow's new communication toys will be? We are full of words, but they come, more and more, through fast-moving fingers on a keyboard. We don't seem to heed James's warning that we should "be swift to hear [and] slow to speak" (James 1:19).

But what comes out of our mouths—and what we might type in a text message or send out on Twitter—is of such vital importance that James devoted twelve entire verses to it. Having just addressed the relationship between our faith and our works, he turned to the relationship between our faith and our words. Our words reveal what is actually within us. Having just made it clear that it's not enough to have the right words without good works, James explained that having good *works* isn't enough if we don't have good *words*.

Recently, I attended a high school reunion. One person I saw hadn't been athletic as a kid. He could not throw a ball or hit one with a bat. Because of this he was the target of some cruel ridicule, taunting, and bullying. When he was young, he generally told his harassers, "Sticks and stones may break my bones, but words will never hurt me."

Through the years, however, I have found that statement untrue. For decades I have worn several scars from sticks and stones. I have a scar on the back of my head from the day a boy up the street bounced a rock off it. I have a scar on my left thigh from the time I was climbing over a picket fence and fell. On my shin is the scar from when a kid slid into second base with his spikes high in the air. All those wounds have healed, and I haven't given one of them a single thought in years. But some people who have been the target of harsh words carry wounds for a lifetime that never heal.

Words have power. They can bless or break; they can help or hurt. Too many children have heard a frustrated parent say, "You are worthless and will never amount to anything." And the children believed it, allowing those words to shape their self-image and determine their self-worth. Other children have had parents affirm them: "You are important, and God has something for you to do that no one can do quite like you can." These children believed that message and ultimately acted on it. Much of who I am today, apart from the saving grace of God, is due to a mom and dad who constantly let me know they were proud of me and that I could do anything if

I set my mind to it and worked hard. The words we say have tremendous power—for good or for bad.

As James addressed the topic of our words, he was echoing what Jesus had said years earlier when rebuking the Pharisees: "For every idle word men may speak, they will give account of it in the day of judgment. For by your words you will be justified and by your words you will be condemned" (Matthew 12:36–37). James made three statements about the use of our tongues, and he gave two illustrations to substantiate each point. First, James reminded people that speech can, in fact, be controlled and directed, and he illustrated his point with a horse bridle and ship rudder. Second, James related that contentious speech can be destructive like fire and poison. Finally, James pointed out that conflicting speech can be deceptive and illustrated this fact with images of a spring of water and a fig tree.

Words define us: they reveal what is in our hearts. Whether we speak words or type them, they have power to heal or to hurt, to help or to hinder.

JUST DO IT! Long years ago I heard a simple, yet profound, comment that I have never forgotten. On uncounted occasions, this statement has rushed into my mind: "You never have to take back what you don't say!" Because words can hurt and harm, James admonished us to "be swift to hear, slow to speak, slow to wrath" (James 1:19). Furthermore, as Jesus warned, "For every idle word that men may speak, they will give account of it in the day of judgment" (Matthew 12:36). Instead of "Just do it!" we need to heed "Just stop it!" You never have to take back what you don't say—or type!

23   CONTROLLED SPEECH CAN BE DIRECTED

My brethren, let not many of you become teachers, knowing that we shall receive a stricter judgment. For we all stumble in many things. If anyone does not stumble in word, he is a perfect man, able also to bridle the whole body. Indeed, we put bits in horses' mouths that they may obey us, and we turn their whole body. Look also at ships: although they are so large and are driven by fierce winds, they are turned by a very small rudder wherever the pilot desires. Even so the tongue is a little member and boasts great things.

—JAMES 3:1–5

AN EXPLANATION

We've all said things we wish we could take back. We've all caused ourselves or others trouble by things we've said. And we've all said things that we can't believe came out of our mouth!

The words we say are formed by our tongue and lips, but those words originate in our hearts. Jesus said, "A good man out of the good treasure of his heart brings forth good; and an evil man out of the evil treasure of his heart brings forth evil. For out of the abundance of the heart his mouth speaks" (Luke 6:45).

And according to James, our words are as important as our works. Like a bridle in a horse's mouth or a rudder on a ship, we can control what we say and use our speech in a way that blesses others. An unbridled tongue, like an unbridled horse, will never accomplish anything worthwhile. But a bridled tongue—like a bridled horse under a master's control—can be very useful. We can actually take control of what we say and use words for our good and the good of others.

AN ILLUSTRATION

James 3:3 is a helpful illustration of the mastery we can have over our tongue: "Indeed, we put bits in horses' mouths that they may obey us, and we turn their whole body." If you have ever bridled a horse, you know that the bridle that slips over the horse's head and behind its ears has a bit, a metal bar that goes in the horse's mouth and lies on top of its tongue. When the rider wants the horse to stop, he pulls back hard on the reins, and the bit presses down on the horse's tongue. The rider who controls the horse's tongue can actually control the horse's whole body—steer it to the right or left, and bring it to a stop with a simple pull on the reins.

A horse controlled by a bit can be of great use, but an unbroken horse can do great damage. Just as a horse needs to come under its master's control, our tongues need to come under our Master's control. A horse can't bridle itself. The one who mastered it puts the bridle on.

My point is that, try as we might, we can't control our tongue through our own efforts. After all, what we say actually originates in our heart, not our mouth. When we yield ourselves under the control of our Master, the Lord Jesus Christ, our speech can honor Him and bless others.

Ships illustrate the same point that horses do: "Look also at ships: although they are so large and are driven by fierce winds, they are turned by a very small rudder wherever the pilot desires." The tongue is like that small rudder: a muscle just a few inches long can build or break someone who is six feet tall.

But back to those rudders. One can't live in Florida, as our family did for fifteen years, without doing some sailing. As James reminded us, it's the wind that propels us along, not the rudder. Winds are necessary. You can't get very far in a sailboat without them. The stronger the winds, the faster the boat moves. However, a sailboat without a rudder is entirely at the mercy of those winds. The boat may go fast, but with nothing to give it direction, it can't easily reach its intended destination.

James's point is clear. A bridle on a horse is of little use unless a rider is in control of the reins. A rudder on a ship is useless unless a captain is at the wheel or stern controlling it.

AN APPLICATION

James went on: "Even so the tongue is a little member and boasts great things." Interestingly, the Greek word we translate "little member" can also mean "melody; the music to which a song is set." God intends our tongues to give life a melody. If the tongue is out of tune, life has no melody. And if we say one thing and do another, the music stops. Our words and our works are meant to blend together in perfect harmony.

Remember, the real issue is not the actual bit in the mouth or the rudder on the ship, but the one who is in control. And I learned something interesting about who is in control of a massive oil tanker when I watched them come in to dock at Port Everglades in Fort Lauderdale. When the tankers are still a ways out of port, a small boat goes out to meet them. On that boat is a man referred to as the "bar pilot." He boards the massive vessel, and the captain who has piloted that huge ship across the ocean steps aside and surrenders the wheel to the bar pilot. That bar pilot knows where the deep channel is cut and where the ship is to be docked. Jesus is our bar pilot, yet too many of us are trying to steer our own ships into the harbor. We need to step aside and surrender to Him the wheel that guides our lives. When we do, our speech will come under His control, and He will direct it in such a way that blesses others and honors Him.

JUST DO IT! Think about the people you know. There's the steady rhythm of some people's lives: they simply live out their days with the same monotonous beat. They have no joy, no energy, no spirit of adventure. They're just existing, in the background, doing the same old thing every day. There's the harmony of other people's lives: they blend in with whoever is around them. They never make any waves and never take the lead; they simply go along with the crowd. And then there are those who give us a melody for life. Their speech is controlled by the Master, so their words are His words and their melody is His melody. The tongue may be a "little member," but we can use it to do great things for God when we surrender it to His control.

24 CONTENTIOUS SPEECH CAN BE DESTRUCTIVE

Even so the tongue is a little member and boasts great things. See how great a forest a little fire kindles! And the tongue is a fire, a world of iniquity. The tongue is so set among our members that it defiles the whole body, and sets on fire the course of nature; and it is set on fire by hell. For every kind of beast and bird, of reptile and creature of the sea, is tamed and has been tamed by mankind. But no man can tame the tongue. It is an unruly evil, full of deadly poison.

—JAMES 3:5–8

AN EXPLANATION

Having spoken about the potential of the tongue to direct speech for the good, James then warned that the same tongue also has potential for evil. Words controlled by our Master can be directed in a positive way, but uncontrolled speech can be contentious and destructive like fire and poison.

I distinctly remember two teachers during my formative school days. My English teacher was a strict disciplinarian. She was up in years, she had never been married, and she had devoted her whole life to instructing young people on the finer points of English grammar and literature. On one occasion, she asked me to stay a moment after class. Assuming I was in some sort of trouble, I did so with apprehension. I approached her desk after all the others had left the room. I could not believe what she said: "Son, you have character, and if you applied yourself in this class, you could be an A student." She believed in me! In fact, that day she changed the way I thought about myself with her simple words of affirmation.

The other teacher I well remember was one of my coaches. He sought to motivate by intimidation, ridicule, and vile words. His goal was to break us down. It didn't work for many of us. More than one kid walked away from that team, head hanging, never to return.

Our words can be controlled or contentious, can be directed in a positive manner or utterly destructive.

AN ILLUSTRATION

People living in Southern California who know the danger of ravaging brush fires driven by desert winds can readily identify with James's words here: "See how great a forest a little fire kindles! And the tongue is a fire, a world of iniquity. The tongue is so set among our members that it defiles the whole body, and sets on fire the course of nature; and it is set on fire by hell." A little spark from a match has started more than one massive fire. Spreading faster and farther than we might ever imagine, that kind of fire destroys millions of dollars of timber and homes, leaving in its wake a scorched landscape.

The tongue, James said, is like a fire. How many reputations have been ruined by a carelessly spoken word? The impact of our words spreads far and fast, especially in our digital age. A word tweeted in Dallas can be retweeted all over the world in seconds. Like a fire, that word can get out of control with lightning speed and do irreparable damage. Contentious speech is always destructive. Like a fire, our words can increase the burning and too often destroy relationships and reputations.

James continued: "For every kind of beast and bird, of reptile and creature of the sea, is tamed and has been tamed by mankind. But no man can tame the tongue." A few years ago while in the East African country of Kenya, I visited the African bush country. I will never forget seeing those proud lions in their natural habitat. It's amazing to think that we have captured these great beasts and trained them to jump through rings of fire and sit on command. Seeing the giant elephants in their natural setting makes it even more difficult to believe that man has trained them to grab each other's tails, march in unison, and stand up on their hind legs on a small box. We can train just about anything there is—except the tongue.

No man can tame his own tongue—but Jesus can! Men can tame and train animals, but it takes a supernatural act of God to tame the sinful human's tongue. God can take a tongue of gossip and turn it into a tongue for glory. He can take a tongue that spews bitterness and turn it into one that speaks blessing.

James had another word to illustrate the destructive potential of the tongue. He said it is "full of deadly poison." Poison usually works secretly and sometimes slowly until it eventually kills. The tongue can be like that. A few poisonous words inserted into a conversation and spoken in venomous antagonism can destroy relationships that were decades in the making and cripple the poisoned person for life. Contentious speech can indeed be immeasurably destructive.

AN APPLICATION

James reminded us that the tongue is destructive like fire or poison and "is set on fire in hell." Behind every spoken word of divisiveness or filth or rumor or anger is Satan himself. This enemy delights in using uncontrolled tongues as a tool as he goes about his business of destroying hearts, homes, and hopes.

Uncontrolled fire can destroy, but fire itself isn't bad. When controlled, it is beneficial. We can heat our homes with it. We can sterilize surgical instruments with it. We can cook our meals with it. In the same way, we can use our words to bless or to blast, to direct or to destroy.

JUST DO IT! We've all had times when we wished we hadn't said what we said and then watched the little spark result in a raging fire we couldn't control. No wonder King David prayed, "Set a guard, O Lord, over my mouth; keep watch over the door of my lips" (Psalm 141:3).

All of us need a guard over our mouth! As I mentioned earlier, for instance, we may find ourselves gossiping (saying behind someone's back what you would never say to his or her face) or flattering (saying to someone's face what you would never say behind his or her back). And both are wrong. So let's join David in asking God to "set a guard over [our] mouth [and] to keep watch over the door of [our] lips."

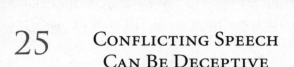

25 CONFLICTING SPEECH CAN BE DECEPTIVE

With [the tongue] we bless our God and Father, and with it we curse men, who have been made in the similitude of God. Out of the same mouth proceed blessing and cursing. My brethren, these things ought not to be so. Does a spring send forth fresh water and bitter from the same opening? Can a fig tree, my brethren, bear olives, or a grapevine bear figs? Thus no spring yields both salt water and fresh.

—JAMES 3:9–12

AN EXPLANATION

While James is known for his teaching that works are evidence of our salvation and genuine faith, he also taught that our words are important. When our words are controlled, they can direct us in right ways. When our words are contentious, they can destroy relationships built over decades or give someone a crippling burden of pain for a lifetime. James also addressed those words that are contradictory and can deceive not only others but ourselves as well. The Native Americans referred to such a person as one who spoke with a "forked tongue." That is, this person said one thing at one time and in one place and the opposite thing at another time and in another place. In James's own words, "These things ought not to be so."

AN ILLUSTRATION

Once more James offered two illustrations to substantiate his point about speech that contradicts itself. First he asked, "Does a spring send forth fresh water and bitter from the same opening?" Many people around the world live in remote villages with no running water. For them it would be a life-giving blessing to live near a spring that bubbles continually with fresh water. But what a disappointment to find a spring of bitter water. Perhaps less useful would be a spring producing both fresh and bitter water: it would be as deceptive as a mouth that speaks both blessings and curses.

James asked this rhetorical question: "Can a fig tree, my brethren, bear olives, or a grapevine bear figs?" Obviously, not a chance. Such inconsistency is impossible in the natural world. Just as the fruit of a tree reveals the health of its root system, so our words reveal what is in our heart. If our hearts are deceitful, our words will be also.

AN APPLICATION

James made it plain: our tongues speak words that spring from our inner nature. Our words reveal who we really are deep inside. Just as it is impossible for saltwater and sweet water to come from the same source and for olives to grow on a fig tree, it is impossible for our tongues to produce what is not in our hearts. If we bless and curse at the same time, something in our heart is desperately out of order. Evil speech emanates from an evil heart. A heart that truly loves God doesn't fuel lies, slanders, gossips, curses, or the like. Jesus said, "Out of the abundance of the heart the mouth speaks" (Matthew 12:34).

We are deceiving ourselves if we think we can go through life speaking with a forked tongue. Our words are a barometer for what is really in our hearts. If our speech is inconsistent, simply washing the mouth out with soap won't work. The remedy must reach much deeper, to the heart. Solutions will never come by trying hard to work on our vocabulary. What we say is not the source of the problem. We can wash our mouths out with soap until the bar of soap is but a sliver and still not solve the problem. Solomon said, "Keep your heart with all diligence, for out of it spring the issues of life" (Proverbs 4:23).

Only an untrained or incompetent physician would treat a symptom and ignore the source of a disease. That's one reason your doctor asks you to stick out your tongue during an examination. Often internal problems can be identified by the film on the tongue. A competent physician, however, would not just clean your tongue off and send you on your way. She would determine the source of your problem rather than just dealing with the symptom.

Those people whose speech is contentious and contradictory too often deal with only the symptoms. They do their best to stop saying things they shouldn't say and try hard

to say the right thing. But no matter how hard we may try, "no man can tame the tongue" (James 3:8). Education can't do it. Turning over yet another new leaf in life can't do it. Nothing in the natural realm can accomplish this. Only a supernatural transformation of the heart can tame a tongue. And that happens to believers because the Christian life is not a changed life; it is an exchanged life. We give God our old life, and He gives us one that is brand-new. This is God's promise: "I will give you a new heart and put a new spirit within you" (Ezekiel 36:26).

Only Christ, through His work on the cross, can truly produce a life of works—and words—that pleases Him and blesses others. Once we have surrendered our will to His, our words and our heart work together in beautiful harmony. As the psalmist requested, "Let the words of my mouth and the meditation of my heart be acceptable in Your sight, O Lord, my strength and my Redeemer" (Psalm 19:14).

Every person has a God-shaped void within his or her heart that can only be filled by Him. That's why the very best thing we can do with our tongues is to confess that Jesus Christ is our Savior and Lord. The Bible says, "If you confess with your mouth the Lord Jesus and believe in your heart that God has raised Him from the dead, you will be saved. For with the heart one believes unto righteousness, and with the mouth confession is made unto salvation" (Romans 10:9–10).

After all, one day every knee will bow and every tongue will confess that "Jesus Christ is Lord, to the glory of God the Father" (Philippians 2:11). Do it now.

JUST DO IT! When living in Florida, we had a giant grapefruit tree in our backyard. That tree produced the most delightful and delicious grapefruit. The secret of that fruit tree was its hidden life: its root system reached deep into the earth, enabling its taproot to connect with sources of hidden water well below the surface. The public life of that fruit tree stood strong because of its hidden but healthy roots. And we are no different. We must find our strength by sending our roots deep into our relationship with God who transforms and fashions our heart. For, as Jesus Himself observed, "Out of the abundance of the heart the mouth speaks" (Matthew 12:34).

26   WISDOM

Who is wise and understanding among you? Let him show by good conduct that his works are done in the meekness of wisdom. But if you have bitter envy and self-seeking in your hearts, do not boast and lie against the truth. This wisdom does not descend from above, but is earthly, sensual, demonic. For where envy and self-seeking exist, confusion and every evil thing are there. But the wisdom that is from above is first pure, then peaceable, gentle, willing to yield, full of mercy and good fruits, without partiality and without hypocrisy. Now the fruit of righteousness is sown in peace by those who make peace.

—JAMES 3:13–18

*W*e live in a world where knowledge is literally at our fingertips and exploding at an exponential pace. The Internet means instant information of global events in real time. When I was young, we had to dig for information. By the time I was a teenager, I had worn out my entire set of *Encyclopædia Britannica*. Today, all that information is available with a simple click of a mouse using any number of free Internet search engines. Many of today's textbooks are out-of-date before the print is even dry. People today have access to more knowledge than at any time in history. Knowledge is readily available to everyone.

Yet wisdom seems practically nonexistent. Paul's words to the Corinthian church could well be addressed to us: "There is not a wise man among you" (1 Corinthians 6:5). Look around at the evidence. Lives are in shambles. Position, power, and prosperity have not brought the peace and purpose they had promised. In our world where so many hopes are smashed and dreams are dashed, we desperately need wisdom.

There is a stark difference between knowledge and wisdom. Knowledge is the accumulation of facts. With dedication to the goal, determination to work hard, and a commitment to the long process, anyone can accumulate facts. Our problem is not accumulating facts. Our problem is our lack of wisdom: we aren't able to take the facts we've learned and put them into practice in real-life situations and at points of need.

James recognized that if we are ever to put our faith into action through good words and good works, we'll need wisdom, and he was quick to point out two sources of wisdom available to us. Natural wisdom is offered by the world's systems and philosophies. Then supernatural wisdom comes from God, and we find it in His Word.

James said the world's wisdom is rooted in the secular, in the sensual, and even in the satanic. Worldly wisdom has contributed to so much of what is wrong with our culture: a drug epidemic, an abortion holocaust, and a national debt of astronomic proportions are only the beginning of a list of the problems that plague our society.

Never have we needed wisdom more than we do today. But the wisdom we need is the wisdom of the Word, not the wisdom of the world. "The wisdom that is from above," said James, "is first pure, then peaceable, gentle, willing to yield, full of mercy and good fruits, without partiality and without hypocrisy." This kind of wisdom is the God-given ability to perceive the true nature of certain circumstances in order to apply His will to the issue at hand. This wisdom only comes from "above."

We all need this kind of wisdom. We need wisdom to know how to provide for our families. Husbands need wisdom to know how to live with our wives "with understanding" (1 Peter 3:7). Parents need wisdom for leading their children in the way they should go (Proverbs 22:6). We all need heaven's wisdom for the myriad decisions we make every day.

Above all, young people today need wisdom. The most important and life-altering decisions aren't made in our more mature years when we have experience and perspective. We make key decisions when we're young. Where will we go to school? What will we study? What vocation will we pursue? Whom shall we marry? We answer these questions and many more like them during our late teen years or early twenties. Tragically, too many of these decisions are made based on the wisdom of the world, not the wisdom of the Word.

Knowing the Lord Jesus Christ in an intimate and personal way gives the believer a great advantage over the unbeliever. The only wisdom nonbelievers have at their disposal is the wisdom of the world that—according to James—at best is "earthly and sensual" and, at worst, "demonic."

Solomon, not yet twenty years of age, was about to be crowned king of Israel. He had to follow in the footsteps of his father, King David, one of the most dynamic and successful leaders in all human history. At this time of his young life, Solomon was pure in mind and virtually void of pride. God asked him, "What shall I give you?" (1 Kings 3:5). That is to say, "What do you want from Me?"

Everyone wants something. Whatever our age, what we *want* may not be what we *need*. However, what we want serves as a very good indicator of where our heart is. Incidentally, there is a greater tragedy than not getting what you want. It is wanting something, getting it, and then finding out it isn't what you really needed after all. We can all tell true stories of people whose lives were ruined because they got what (or whom) they wanted only to find that the wisdom of the world did not lead to the fulfillment they had hoped.

When God asked Solomon what he wanted, Solomon had the right answer. His priorities were in the right order. He didn't have to ponder or think long and hard about his answer. Right away he requested, "Give to Your servant an understanding heart . . . that I may discern between good and evil" (1 Kings 3:9). Solomon desired the wisdom that comes from above, not wisdom from the world, so he asked God for wisdom. Solomon recognized the lack of wisdom to be his greatest need. Years later, when penning one of his proverbs, he wrote, "Wisdom is the principal thing; therefore get wisdom. And in all your getting, get understanding" (Proverbs 4:7).

JUST DO IT! If God were to ask you right now, "What do you want Me to give you?" what would you say? Decide now to do as Solomon did and ask for wisdom, the wisdom from above. Ask God to work *with* you, to work *in* you, and to work *through* you to make you a person of wisdom. As you pray, remember James's earlier challenge and promise: "If any of you lacks wisdom, let him ask of God, who gives to all liberally and without reproach, and it will be given to him" (James 1:5).

27 The WISDOM of the WORLD

Who is wise and understanding among you? Let him show by good conduct that his works are done in the meekness of wisdom. But if you have bitter envy and self-seeking in your hearts, do not boast and lie against the truth. This wisdom does not descend from above, but is earthly, sensual, demonic. For where envy and self-seeking exist, confusion and every evil thing are there.

—JAMES 3:13–16

ITS ORIGIN

*J*ames left no doubt about the origin of worldly wisdom. It "does not descend from above, but is earthly, sensual, demonic." In Christian theology, this unholy trinity of spiritual enemies has come to be called the world, the flesh, and the Devil. The apostle John referred to these three as "the lust of the flesh, the lust of the eyes, and the pride of life" (1 John 2:16). One thing is sure: this worldly wisdom is not from God.

The wisdom of the world originates in the *secular*: it is "earthly." And this earthly wisdom originates in the secular world where our minds are set solely on earthly things, and confusion results. Genesis 11 is a prime example. In a quest to make a name for themselves, these descendants of

Noah chose secular wisdom. Acting according to humanistic, earthly thinking, they built a tower to reach to heaven. It seemed to them like a good thing to do, but the result of that construction project was mass confusion.

Like the crowd at Babel, King Saul based his decisions on earthly reasoning and human wisdom. He thought, for instance, it would be wise to put his armor on young David before he faced the giant of Gath, Goliath. The armor didn't fit David, and it wouldn't help him. In contrast to Saul, young David was guided by the wisdom of God's Word, and he fought in the strength of the Lord (1 Samuel 17:37, 45–46). Too often we make decisions the same way Saul did. Earthly, worldly wisdom, with its roots in the secular system around us, will never serve us as well as heavenly, divine wisdom.

In addition to having these secular roots, the wisdom of the world is also rooted in the *sensual*. We actually derive part of our English word *psychology* from the same Greek root from which we translate the word *sensual* in James 3:15, referring to that part of us that animates the body. The ancients believed a human being was divided into three parts; body, soul, and spirit. The body is comprised of our flesh and bones, the soul animates the body and gives expression to our personality, and the spirit is that part of us that will live as long as God lives. Only we humans possess a spirit that can be in relationship with God, and this separates us from all the other created order. You and I have the capacity to connect with God, spirit to Spirit, and to know Him in the intimacy of a father and his child. What an awesome reality!

So, in describing the wisdom of the world as "sensual," James was saying that it is the kind of wisdom that animals use. This wisdom is based on nothing more than our natural or animal instincts. With little thought of anything except personal survival, we make our decisions solely on the basis of the senses, the sensual. Could it be, then, that at the root of some mental illness is the neglect of the spiritual part of us that can only be made right by God? The wisdom of the world that originates in the secular and the sensual ignores the spirit.

The fact that worldly wisdom is based in part on our senses explains why so many people live by "If it feels good, do it." This guideline for life gives priority to feelings over faith. It is sensual at its root: "I will believe it when I see it . . . or touch it . . . or smell it . . . or taste it . . . or hear it." Worldly wisdom has no place for the Spirit. Worldly wisdom cannot connect man with God, so it can't be the source of true wisdom.

Worldly wisdom is fueled by the secular, the sensual, and, finally, the *satanic*—or, to use James's word, the "demonic." Rather than a mere insinuation or even a strong accusation, this is a fact. As the ruler of this world, Satan is ultimately behind its so-called wisdom.

To find the beginning of the world's wisdom, we must journey back to Eden where Satan slithered in to deceive Eve. He used the wisdom of the world in place of the wisdom of God's promises to her. Earlier God had warned, "Of every tree of the garden you may freely eat; but the tree of the knowledge of good and evil you shall not eat, for in the day that you eat of it you shall surely die" (Genesis 2:16–17). Then came the satanic untruth of the world: "You will not surely die" (3:4). Eve made a choice: figuring that eating from the tree was "desirable to make one wise" (v. 6), she chose the world's way. And the result? Exactly as James described: "envy and self-seeking . . . confusion and every evil thing" became Eve's lot in life.

How did it happen? As we've seen, Satan's deceit brings a selfish desire that leads to a sinful decision that ultimately results in a sure defeat.

ITS OUTCOME

Following the wisdom of the world will result in envy, which is defined as "the displeasure we take in someone else's good fortune." When God accepted Abel's sacrifice, envy motivated his brother, Cain, to kill him. Envy motivated Joseph's brothers to throw him in a pit and sell him to the Ishmaelites, who in turn sold him into Egyptian slavery.

Another outcome of applying only worldly wisdom is what James referred to as "self-seeking." Paul talked about "selfish ambition," a phrase that describes those who pursue an office in a self-seeking way. In order to get elected, they will say anything they need to anyone anywhere and at any time. People motivated by selfish ambition will plot, scheme, connive, and use any means necessary to gain their end result. And a disapproving Paul countered, "Let nothing be done through selfish ambition or conceit, but in lowliness of mind let each esteem others as better than himself" (Philippians 2:3).

In addition to envy and self-seeking, confusion and disorder also result from the world's wisdom. Instead of bringing people together, it divides people and tears individuals apart. Paul reminded the Corinthians—and us—that "God is not the author of confusion" (1 Corinthians 14:33). Confusion is the natural result of the wisdom that originates in the world.

Finally, James related that the world's wisdom results in "every evil thing." This wisdom—the guide for so many people today—brings no ultimate good. It results only in "envy and self-seeking . . . confusion and every evil thing."

We don't have to teach our children the wisdom of the world. We never have to teach our kids to disobey, to say no, or to grab a toy from a playmate. They, like all of us, were born with a tendency to follow the wisdom of this world. Simply put, they were born with a sin nature. And that's the reason we have to teach our children to obey, not to disobey. We have to teach them to talk kindly, not talk back. We have to teach them to share, not hoard. We have to teach them the better way, the wisdom that comes from above, the wisdom of the Word.

JUST DO IT! Why do you think the theory of evolution is so popular among secularists and so widely accepted by academia? It is certainly not popular because it's supported by any scientific data. There is little, if any, real evidence supporting evolution. Could this theory be popular because its origin is in the secular, the sensual, the satanic? Could it be the Devil's attempt to explain the existence of everything without giving God any credit at all? Consider the miracle of childbirth. Could two tiny bits of protoplasm, too small to be seen by the naked eye, come together and result in a living being with a nervous system, a respiratory system, a circulatory system, a reproductive system, and a digestive system really be the result of mere chance? The wisdom of the world will never sufficiently answer life's greatest questions or solve life's greatest riddles. We need wisdom from above.

28 *The* WISDOM *of the* WORD

But the wisdom that is from above is first pure, then peaceable, gentle, willing to yield, full of mercy and good fruits, without partiality and without hypocrisy. Now the fruit of righteousness is sown in peace by those who make peace.

—JAMES 3:17–18

ITS ORIGIN

The word *but* that begins verse 17 is not there by accident. Having just described the nature of worldly wisdom, James next contrasted it with the wisdom from above. This wisdom of the Word comes from God, and He enables us to apply His wisdom to our earthly challenges.

This wisdom of the Word has a divine origin. It comes "from above." Wise Solomon put it thus: "The Lord gives wisdom; from His mouth come knowledge and understanding" (Proverbs 2:6). Wisdom is God's supernatural gift to any and all of us who ask Him for it. Paul acknowledged God as the source of wisdom when praying for his brothers and sisters in the faith at Ephesus. The apostle prayed "that the God of our Lord Jesus Christ, the Father of glory, may give to you the spirit of wisdom and revelation in the knowledge of Him"

(Ephesians 1:17). And for his Colossian friends, Paul asked that God would fill them with "the knowledge of His will in all wisdom and spiritual understanding" (Colossians 1:9).

The wisdom of the Word is God's special gift, supernaturally bestowed on His people. The only requirement is that we ask God for it (see James 1:5). We won't find godly wisdom through any kind of education or practical experience. After all, it isn't learned. James laid it out: "If any of you lacks wisdom, let him ask of God, who gives to all liberally and without reproach, and it will be given to him. But let him ask in faith, with no doubting, for he who doubts is like a wave of the sea driven and tossed by the wind" (James 1:5–6). Wisdom from above is God's gift, freely given to those who simply ask. But we must ask in faith, believing God will hear our prayer and provide.

This wisdom comes to us by the living Word—by the Lord Jesus Christ Himself, who is "the power of God and the wisdom of God . . . [and] who became for us wisdom from God" (1 Corinthians 1:24, 30). Without Christ, who is the very wisdom of God incarnate, we have no hope of gaining heaven's wisdom for our daily needs. Thus, our first step in finding wisdom is to come to know Jesus as a personal Savior and Lord and put our trust totally in Him. (See Epilogue on page 275.)

Godly wisdom also comes to us by way of the written Word, the Bible. This is why Paul—in his last letter before being beheaded for the gospel—wrote to young Timothy and said, "From childhood you have known the Holy Scriptures, which are able to make you wise" (2 Timothy 3:15). This wisdom from above is modeled by the living Word and set forth in the written Word, and God is glorified in both.

ITS OUTCOME

When we begin to apply heaven's wisdom in our lives, purity—or spiritual integrity—results. The wisdom of the world brings perversion, but godly wisdom results in purity. We don't become pure through our own good works or efforts. We only become pure before God through the blood of Jesus and His finished work on our behalf on the cross. And wisdom enables us to live out that purity.

A pure person will be, to use James's word, "peaceable": he will be a promoter of peace. Jesus didn't pronounce a blessing on the peace *lovers* in the Beatitudes but on the peace*makers* (Matthew 5:9). Christ blesses the active promoters of unity and peace.

Another benefit that comes when we apply the wisdom of God to our lives is patience—or, to use James's word, "gentleness." With it comes a willingness to yield. This person shows consideration for others, an exact opposite of the envy we see in those who only apply worldly wisdom.

Next, James referred to being "full of mercy." God's wisdom is characterized by an abundance of mercy and forgiveness. It may take two to start a quarrel or a fight, but it only takes one person applying heaven's wisdom to the situation to stop it.

Then James added "full of good fruits." Jesus reminded us that His true followers will be known "by their fruits" (Matthew 7:20).

And, finally, heaven's wisdom results in our being "without partiality and without hypocrisy." In ancient Greek drama, one actor would play several different roles. When changing from one character to another, he would hold different masks to his face. In some cases, the actor would be both hero and villain in the same play. Such an actor was called a "hypocrite." Over the years this word has come to describe a two-faced individual hiding behind the mask of a false life. He pretends to be something he is not. James was telling us that people living according to wisdom from above don't hide behind a mask and don't pretend to be someone they're not. Heaven's wisdom is "without hypocrisy."

The wisdom of the Word can change your life. Each of us must choose between the wisdom of the world and the wisdom of the Word. We aren't puppets; we are people, and the choice is ours to make. Just know that the wisest decision anyone ever makes is to line up on God's side.

JUST DO IT! "Who is wise and understanding among you?" (James 3:13). That is a good question. Some of us have understanding and knowledge. We know facts, but we have little wisdom or discernment to help us make wise decisions. We've all encountered individuals whose intelligence borders on genius, yet who make so many unwise choices that they can hardly manage their lives. Still other people may be discerning in spirit, but they don't equip themselves with basic knowledge they need for life.

Knowledge is the accumulation of facts. Wisdom is the ability to take those facts and apply them to everyday situations. It's hard to apply the Bible's truth to life if we don't have a working and accurate knowledge of it: we need to know what Scripture actually says. Also, asking for wisdom does not eliminate our need to study God's Word. In fact, our desire for wisdom should fuel our desire for greater knowledge of God. Wisdom and knowledge, like ham and eggs or steak and potatoes, go together. Both wisdom and knowledge are important, but wisdom is essential.

WAR *and* PEACE

Where do wars and fights come from among you? Do they not come from your desires for pleasure that war in your members? You lust and do not have. You murder and covet and cannot obtain. You fight and war. Yet you do not have because you do not ask. You ask and do not receive, because you ask amiss, that you may spend it on your pleasures. Adulterers and adulteresses! Do you not know that friendship with the world is enmity with God? Whoever therefore wants to be a friend of the world makes himself an enemy of God. Or do you think that the Scripture says in vain, "The Spirit who dwells in us yearns jealously"? But He gives more grace. Therefore He says: "God resists the proud, but gives grace to the humble." Therefore submit to God. Resist the devil and he will flee from you. Draw near to God and He will draw near to you. Cleanse your hands, you sinners; and purify your hearts, you double-minded. Lament and mourn and weep! Let your laughter be turned to mourning and your joy to gloom. Humble yourselves in the sight of the Lord, and He will lift you up. Do not speak evil of one another, brethren. He who speaks evil of a brother and judges his brother, speaks evil of the law and judges the law. But if you judge the law, you are not a doer of the law but a judge. There is one Lawgiver, who is able to save and to destroy. Who are you to judge another?

—JAMES 4:1–12

"Where do wars and fights come from among you?" James asked. Our current world situation makes this opening question as relevant as it has been in any generation. War has existed in every era of human existence. No civilization has been untouched. Our Lord warned of "wars and rumors of wars" (Matthew 24:6). In the 5,600 years of recorded human history, approximately 15,000 wars have been fought. And as General Sherman, the Union leader who burned Confederate cities on his march to the sea, said, "War is hell."*

We all know the ravages of war. We might not know the fear and fatigue of being in a foxhole in enemy territory, but we know, for instance, the struggle of private wars that flare up within us as the flesh wars against the spirit. We know personal wars that have torn asunder close relationships. And there are public wars waged on a large and sometimes global scale. Whether wars are private, personal, or public in nature, they have common symptoms, sources, and even solutions.

First of all, most of us know what it is to be engaged in a private war that rages within us. Perhaps few, if anyone, will know it is taking place. But we do. Paul himself was engaged in a private war. He struggled. He fought. He framed it like this: "What I am doing, I do not understand. For what I will to do, that I do not practice; but what I hate, that I do" (Romans 7:15). We all have this same testimony. All too often we find ourselves not doing what we know we should and doing the very things we know we should not. Describing this internal conflict, Paul said, "The flesh lusts against the Spirit, and the

Spirit against the flesh; and these are contrary to one another, so that you do not do the things that you wish" (Galatians 5:17). We have all experienced this private, internal conflict.

But we are fighting other wars as well. We also know the turmoil of personal wars. These wars crop up when interpersonal relationships become frayed for one reason or another. Our current culture is no stranger to these personal wars. Husbands war against wives. At the office, healthy competition can turn into hostile jealousies. Children war against their parents. Former friends war against one another. Almost forgotten is the admonition from Christ that if we come to worship Him and remember that someone has something against us, we should first go and be reconciled by mending the broken relationship and then worship Him (Matthew 5:23–25).

Then there are the public wars that rage around the globe, holding people hostage in encounters that have paralyzing effects. In the past it was a bit easier to identify these public conflicts because they involved nation against nation. The United States fought against Germany in the European Theatre and against Japan in the South Pacific in World War II. We engaged North Korea in the early 1950s, entered Vietnam in the 1970s, and fought the Cold War with Russia until the 1990s. But today we are embroiled in a new type of war: a war on terror. As I pen these very words, today's news tells of a radical Islamic terror group that has just executed thirteen teenagers in Mosul for breaking sharia law. Their crime? They were watching a soccer match on television. Wars are raging all around us—some are private, some personal, and some quite public.

The Bible tells us that in the last days there will be an escalation of wars, eventually culminating in the final and climactic battle of mankind: Armageddon. It may not be a coincidence that events today—events that are potentially leading up to this final conflict—are transpiring in the exact geographical spot foretold by biblical prophets thousands of years ago. The continuing hostilities in the Middle East will never be settled at negotiating tables. The roots of this ongoing conflict are firmly planted in centuries of ethnic hatred and hostility. Middle Eastern Bedouins are no longer riding camels and firing single-shot rifles. They are flying supersonic fighter planes, manning sophisticated underground missile systems, and, in some cases, wearing body bombs. And, in their minds, all is justified in the name of *jihad*, or holy war.

Again, the stage may well be being set for Armageddon and Christ's return. A growing number of Bible scholars believe the curtain is about to rise on the final act of mankind. Ours is a world standing on the brink of an apocalyptic war. So James's question has never been more timely: "Where do wars and fights come from among you?" He is about to reveal to us war's symptoms and its sources. But he doesn't stop there. He provides a solution. Let's read on.

JUST DO IT! Those of us who sit in the comfort and safety of our Western world homes may feel far removed from war. But we aren't. Wars aren't limited to global and regional conflicts. Some of us war within ourselves. The very thing we don't want to do, we too often end up doing. And the thing we know we ought to do, we too often leave undone. Our flesh wars internally against our spirit. Others may be at war with someone else, a war that may result in a broken relationship. Worse, some people may be at war with God Himself. James said, "God resists the proud, but gives grace to the humble." Would you like to get on the other side of these conflicts? "Humble yourselves in the sight of the Lord, and He will lift you up" (James 4:10). Our God is rich in grace.

*This quote originates from General Sherman's address to the graduating class of the Michigan Military Academy (19 June 1879).

30   WAR HAS ITS SYMPTOMS

Where do wars and fights come from among you? Do they not come from your desires for pleasure that war in your members? You lust and do not have. You murder and covet and cannot obtain. You fight and war. Yet you do not have because you do not ask. You ask and do not receive, because you ask amiss, that you may spend it on your pleasures.

—JAMES 4:1–3

*T*here is a vast difference between symptoms and sources. For example, we do not get over a flu virus (the source of sickness) by simply treating a runny nose (the symptom). The believers to whom James was writing were engaged in a war of words. He admonished them to "not speak evil of one another" (James 4:11). Their words were not the root cause of the conflict; they were external symptoms of something deeper within.

Too often in our everyday lives, we seek to mend relationships by dealing only with symptoms. The suppressed anger that lurks behind many verbal outbursts, for instance, is left untouched as we seek to discipline our children for their words or to mend relationships we have jeopardized with our own words.

Why are we at war with one another? Where do these personal and private wars come from? In most cases we are at war with someone else because we are at war with ourselves. We experience relationships in three different directions. We have *outward* relationships with people at home, at the office, or in the social arena. We each have an *inward* relationship with ourselves. Some call it self-worth or self-esteem. The third relationship we have separates us from the rest of the created order: we have the capacity for an *upward* relationship with God through the Lord Jesus Christ.

Essential to understand, however, is the truth that we are never properly related to others until we are properly related to ourselves. And none of us will ever be properly related to our self until we discover how indescribably valuable we are to God and enter a personal and life-giving relationship with Him. So wars continue to rage in many of our relationships because, instead of dealing with sources of the problems, we spend our time and effort dealing with symptoms.

And the source of our relationship problems? It lies within us. Thus, on the heels of James's inquiry as to where the "wars and fights" come from, he asked a second question: "Do they not come from your desires for pleasure that war in your members?"

In some ways a Christian is a civil war incarnate. That is why Paul observed, "The flesh lusts against the Spirit, and the Spirit against the flesh; and these are contrary to one another, so that you do not do the things that you wish" (Galatians 5:17). We all know this internal conflict. A part of us fights to

exalt itself; the other resists and seeks humility instead.

For many in our culture, life has become a competitive arena. An insatiable desire and lust for such things as possessions, power, popularity, position, and the like seek to take over, and such selfishness leads to many wrongs. James continued: "You lust and do not have. You murder and covet and cannot obtain. You fight and war." All this turmoil leads us to stop asking for the right things: "You do not have because you do not ask." And even those who ask do not get answers because of the selfish motive behind their requests: "You ask and do not receive, because you ask amiss, that you may spend it on your pleasures."

War of any kind and on every scale always finds its origin in selfish desire. It doesn't matter whether it is a global war, a gang war, a family feud, or a cold war of words. Selfish desire—as we have already seen with Adam and Eve and King David—is always at the root. The apostle Paul knew this struggle and even testified to his own inner fight: "We ourselves were also once foolish, disobedient, deceived, serving various lusts and pleasures, living in malice and envy, hateful and hating one another" (Titus 3:3).

In the fleshly realm there is a part of us that always wants what we do not have. Some of us want something that belongs to someone else—his job, his opportunity, even his wife. For those of us who are at war within ourselves, driven by desires that are outside God's boundaries, there seems never to be enough. Ask those possessed by money, "How much is enough?" No matter how much they have, the reply will be,

"Just a little more." Ask someone consumed with lust or sex and the answer is the same: "Just a little more." Some people are consumed by popularity. Ask them how much is enough. They will say, "Just a little more. Just another pat on the back. Just another round of applause." There is never enough to fill the void of the human heart. Worldly things will never permanently satisfy the human heart.

And this selfish desire James referred to causes wars among us. But the war is simply an external symptom, not the source. Many interpersonal relationships are never healed because we focus on the externals—on the fight—rather than the real issue. In other words, all the outward manifestations of conflict are but symptoms of a problem that has its source within us. The outward sins of David and Bathsheba that resulted in such hurt, humiliation, and even death began within David's own heart: he selfishly desired to have someone who belonged to someone else. Yes, wars and fights are but symptoms. The real problem lies within the selfish desires of our hearts.

JUST DO IT! As the old spiritual goes, "Not my brother, not my sister, but it's me, O Lord, standin' in the need of prayer." But some of us don't pray. We don't even ask God for help. Others of us pray but with the wrong motives. God answers prayer. So pray! Sometimes His answer will be *direct* and immediate. Sometimes it is *delayed.* For His own good reasons, He keeps us in a holding pattern until, for instance, we learn some life lessons. At other times our request is *denied*. I, for one, am thankful God has not granted me everything I've prayed for—because I later realized I was much better off without. Then there are times when God's answer is *different* from what I expected. Why? For my good and for His glory.

31   WAR HAS ITS SOURCES

Adulterers and adulteresses! Do you not know that friendship with the world is enmity with God? Whoever therefore wants to be a friend of the world makes himself an enemy of God. Or do you think that the Scripture says in vain, "The Spirit who dwells in us yearns jealously"? But He gives more grace. Therefore He says: "God resists the proud, but gives grace to the humble."

—JAMES 4:4–6

The real source of our personal and private conflicts lies not in the relationships we have with others or even in the relationship we have with our own selves. The wellspring of our external conflicts is found in our own rebellious relationship with God. James pointed specifically to our selfish desires that continually cause conflict. We constantly fight to have our own way. It is not an oversimplification to say that rebellion against God in the human heart is the root cause of every war, whether its battlefield is the home, the heart, or the other side of the earth.

James was clear: when we choose to be a "friend of the world," we are choosing to be an enemy of God. After all, the prevailing world system of thought—"the world"—is utterly anti-God and anti-Christ. When we aren't on our spiritual guard, we can develop an affection for the things of the world that God says we should avoid.

A friendship with the world can ultimately lead to a love for the world and what it offers. That's why, in one of his New Testament letters, the apostle John warned, "Do not love the world or the things in the world. If anyone loves the world, the love of the Father is not in him" (1 John 2:15). Do not be mistaken. There is no demilitarized zone for Christians who are out of fellowship with God. If you are a friend of the world, you are an enemy of God. There is no place for you to take refuge.

Some ancient manuscripts omit James's use of *adulterers* in verse 4 but leave the word *adulteresses*. But James was not singling out only women here. Men are just as guilty of spiritual adultery. James's emphasis on the feminine here is because he was talking about the bride of Christ, the church: you and me.

Are any of us guilty of this charge of spiritual adultery? Perhaps we once came to an altar and made a pledge openly and publicly to Christ. Surely we should have been as faithful to Him as we have been to our own husbands or wives. But in becoming "friends with the world," we have sought the affection of such other gods as materialism or popularity. When we begin to desire the things of the world more than we desire the things of God, we commit spiritual adultery. We become like married spouses who begin to flirt and are ultimately seduced by other men or women.

Spiritual adultery was the sin of the church at Ephesus, to

whom Jesus said, "I have this against you, that you have left your first love. Remember therefore from where you have fallen; repent and do the first works, or else I will come to you quickly and remove your lampstand from its place—unless you repent" (Revelation 2:4–5). This may be one of the most misquoted verses in Scripture. Jesus did not say we had *lost* our first love; He said we had "left" it. I would much rather admit I lost something than admit I left it behind. To leave something implies greater personal responsibility. We have a faithful and loving husband in the Lord Jesus Christ who always has our best interest in mind. Why would we choose to be at war with Him who seeks only to provide for us and protect us?

One more thing. I don't believe James was speaking softly in these verses. I think he was shouting when he said, "Do you think that the Scripture says in vain, 'The Spirit who dwells in us yearns jealously'"? He was expressing shock and surprise at those individuals who had embraced Christ, known His love, and now were flirting with the world around them. Essentially James was saying—and saying loudly—"What are you thinking? Have you left behind your moral compass? Don't you know that your God is a jealous God?"

But James didn't leave us there. Remembering the words of wise King Solomon, recorded in Proverbs 3:34, James added, "God resists the proud, but gives grace to the humble." Our God is the God of the second chance. Our own internal wars can come to an end once we humble ourselves before God. We have this promise from Christ's own lips: "He who humbles himself will be exalted" (Matthew 23:12).

In light of all this, we do have hope: "He gives more grace." This is the most beautiful phrase in James's entire letter. Poet Annie Johnson Flint (1866–1932) said it well long years ago:

> His love has no limit; His grace has no measure,
> His power has no boundary known unto men.
> For out of His infinite riches in Jesus,
> He giveth, and giveth, and giveth again!

As James said, "He gives more grace." And the only reason we don't have that grace is that we haven't asked!

JUST DO IT! Wars and conflicts arise because we have "left [our] first love" (Revelation 2:4). We never *lose* our love for Christ if we have ever had it. But we can *leave* it. Jesus, in making this accusation, also revealed the threefold way of recovering that love: "Remember therefore from where you have fallen; repent and do the first works" (Revelation 2:5). *Remember*. Where did you leave that love? Go back to the spot. *Repent*. Change your mind. A true change of mind will result in a change of your will, which will then change your actions. *Renew*. "Do the first works." Start doing what you once did. It is much easier to act your way into a new way of feeling than to feel your way into a new way of acting.

32   War Has Its Solutions

Therefore submit to God. Resist the devil and he will flee from you. Draw near to God and He will draw near to you. Cleanse your hands, you sinners; and purify your hearts, you double-minded. Lament and mourn and weep! Let your laughter be turned to mourning and your joy to gloom. Humble yourselves in the sight of the Lord, and He will lift you up. Do not speak evil of one another, brethren. He who speaks evil of a brother and judges his brother, speaks evil of the law and judges the law. But if you judge the law, you are not a doer of the law but a judge. There is one Lawgiver, who is able to save and to destroy. Who are you to judge another?

—JAMES 4:7–12

*J*esus Christ, the Prince of Peace, is the solution to all our wars. Whether it is a cosmic conflict or a family fight, He is the only true and eternal solution to war. This world will never find peace without embracing the Prince of Peace. This may sound simplistic to some people, but it's true. History continues to testify to wars and to spawn ever-increasing rumors of wars. But there is a day coming when Christ will return to usher in a millennium of peace upon this war-weary world. In that day, as Isaiah foretold, our swords will be beaten into plowshares and the lion will lie down peaceably beside the lamb (Isaiah 2:4; 11:6).

James concluded his words on war and conflict with a series of five verbs, all of which are in the imperative tense, signifying that these are not options, but commands. In essence they are five stepping stones that lead to a life of inner peace: "submit . . . resist . . . draw near . . . cleanse . . . humble yourselves."

The first step is *submission*. James began, "Submit to God. Resist the devil and he will flee from you." Many of us have read this verse, rushed out to resist the Devil, and failed every time. Why? Because resistance has a prerequisite: "submit to God." *To submit* literally means to "line up under." James was saying that the first step toward peace is to put ourselves under the lordship of Jesus Christ. This is an act of our will that precludes having our own way. It becomes His way, not our way; His will, not our will. It is akin to Christ's own prayer on the evening before the crucifixion: "Not My will, but Yours, be done" (Luke 22:42).

The next step is *opposition*. James challenged us to oppose evil, to "resist the devil." The moment we submit to Christ, we have a new enemy in Satan, but we can resist him. This Greek word means "to stand against," and this is a military phrase meaning to "take your stand against someone or something."

James was revealing to us the defensive aspect of our fight against the enemy: we are to resist. Paul spoke of this from prison in Rome when he wrote, "Take up the whole armor of God, that you may be able to withstand in the evil day, and having done all, to stand. Stand therefore, having girded your

169

waist with truth, having put on the breastplate of righteousness" (Ephesians 6:13–14).

Many of us are fooled by the demonic deceiver, but this enemy is not the problem. We are. Consider this promise: when you submit to God, clothe yourself in His armor, and resist the Devil, "he will flee from you." Do we really believe that? We definitely would if we remembered he is already a defeated foe. The apostle John attested to this when he said, "You are of God, little children, and . . . He who is in you is greater than he who is in the world" (1 John 4:4). While Satan may be a "roaring lion," that is all he can do. He can only roar; he has no teeth. Satan's doom is sealed. Jesus said, "All authority has been given to Me in heaven and on earth" (Matthew 28:18). Since Jesus has been given "all" authority, Satan has none. N-O-N-E! The only authority Satan has over you is what you yield to him when you refuse to submit to God.

Again, the first two steps toward inner peace are to "submit to God" and "resist the devil." Next comes an interesting *proposition*: "Draw near to God and He will draw near to you." There is only one way we can approach God, much less come near to Him, and that is through the blood of His Son, our Lord Jesus Christ. This is why Paul said, "In Christ Jesus you who once were far off have been brought near by the blood of Christ" (Ephesians 2:13).

James was writing to believers, so he was not necessarily referring to salvation. Instead he was addressing the need of those Christians living in sin to repent. He was addressing those who are torn between the wisdom of the world and the

170

wisdom of the Word. Most of us remember the story of the prodigal son. Longfellow referred to it as the greatest short story ever told. The wayward lad "drew near" to his faithful and forgiving father, and then the father drew near to him.

The fourth step involves an *admonition*. We must admit our need for forgiveness and ask God for it: "Cleanse your hands, you sinners; and purify your hearts, you double-minded. Lament and mourn and weep!" True sorrow for our sin is essential for repentance.

Cleansing our hands has to do with repenting and turning away from our unhealthy and unwise external actions. Purifying our hearts has to do with repenting of our ungodly internal attitudes. The actions of our hands are always a result of the attitudes of our hearts.

Clean hands and a pure heart are key to drawing near to God. That is why the psalmist asked, "Who may ascend into the hill of the Lord? . . . He who has clean hands and a pure heart" (Psalm 24:3–4). That hill is Mount Calvary. Who can ascend there? I can't. Only one person ever lived who could ascend this hill of sacrifice and substitution. That person was Jesus, the only One who lived a spotless life. But on that hill, His consistently clean hands became dirty when He took on my sin and yours, and His always-pure heart became impure so that our impure hearts could be made pure.

Finally, there is a *disposition*. James said, "Humble yourselves in the sight of the Lord and He will lift you up." In the Greek this sentence is in the passive voice, indicating that the subject does not act, but is acted upon. The point is God lifts

us up; we can't lift up ourselves. To humble ourselves before God is to recognize our bankrupt spiritual condition and to admit our need of Him. How much more satisfying to have Christ exalt us before others than to seek to exalt ourselves! Yes, "God resists the proud, but gives grace to the humble" (James 4:6). God hates the sin of pride (Proverbs 6:16–17) and battles against it. But the good news is this: God is rich in grace toward those who humble themselves before Him.

JUST DO IT!
There will never be peace on an international level until there is peace on a national level. There will never be peace in a nation until there is peace on the state level. And peace at the state level won't happen until there is peace on the county level, which in turn will not happen without peace at the city level. We will never have peace at the city level until we know peace in our own community. Our community won't know peace until we have peace on our streets. And we can't have peace on our streets until we have peace on our block. We can't have peace on our block until we have peace in our own home. And we will never have peace in our home until we have peace with God in our own hearts through our personal faith in Jesus Christ. So let us "draw near to God and He will draw near to [us]."

33   ROOTS *of* RECESSION: *The* ARROGANCE *of* OUR AGE

Come now, you who say, "Today or tomorrow we will go to such and such a city, spend a year there, buy and sell, and make a profit"; whereas you do not know what will happen tomorrow. For what is your life? It is even a vapor that appears for a little time and then vanishes away. Instead you ought to say, "If the Lord wills, we shall live and do this or that." But now you boast in your arrogance. All such boasting is evil. Therefore, to him who knows to do good and does not do it, to him it is sin.

—JAMES 4:13–17

*R*ecession. The very word sends chills up a business owner's back. Ask any broker or banker to give you a one-sentence definition of this recurring dilemma of our western economy, and you will get answers such as these:

- A recession is two consecutive down quarters in the gross domestic product.

- A recession is an economic decline brought about by higher unemployment, declining consumer purchasing, tightening credit, and an overall slump in the economy.

Still another answer would be along these lines:

- A recession is a consistent decline in overall economic activity resulting in the loss of jobs. (This definition can be fine-tuned: a recession is when your neighbor is out of work, and a depression is when you are out of work.)

- And, according to Webster's, a recession is "a period of reduced economic activity, a receding, a withdrawal."

When economic recessions come, the blame game begins. People blame the president and his policies. Others blame Congress. Democrats blame Republicans, and Republicans blame Democrats. Some people blame unions. Others place the blame on major financial scandals or a Middle Eastern oil crisis. Ask a dozen people in Washington, DC, what brings on a recession, and you are likely to get a dozen different answers. Perhaps the apostle James got closest to the real answer.

In this section of verses, James was interested not in economic recessions, but in the spiritual recessions that plague many of our hearts and homes. Remember that a recession is a withdrawal, a period of reduced activity, and this can happen in our spiritual lives. There is a sense in which our spiritual lives are like the stock market. We have periods when we are riding the crest of spiritual momentum, seemingly reaching new highs with the wind at our back. But if we are honest, we all have times of declining interest when life's pressures and even Satan's forces seem to hold us down spiritually. All of us know the meaning of a spiritual recession.

The roots of spiritual recession are the same as the roots

of any other kind of recession. According to James, the roots are threefold. Spiritual recession in your life and mine can result from *foolish presumptions*. Too often too many of us presume that we'll never have to deal with the consequences of our sin. Spiritual recession can also result from *forgotten perspectives*. That's why James reminded us that our lives are like "a vapor that appears for a little time and then vanishes away." Spiritual recession can also occur because of *forsaken priorities*. In James's words, "To him who knows to do good and does not do it, to him it is sin."

James began this passage by getting our attention: "Come now you who say . . ." Perhaps a better translation would be simply, "Now listen!" In Greek, the language of the New Testament, this second-person singular pronoun indicates that James was now speaking to you or me individually. He was not talking to the crowd or the congregation. He was talking to you and, in essence, saying, "Stop thinking these words are written for someone else. That is arrogance and presumption. These words are for you." Once James had our attention, he revealed the taproot of recession: the arrogance of our age. But that's not all. James also gave us some really good advice for life and living.

JUST DO IT!

I am very fortunate in that I am seldom sick. However, sometime ago I got up in the middle of the night feeling extremely nauseous. I stumbled into the bathroom, opened the medicine cabinet, and there it was. That pink bottle. I hate the taste of that stuff, but desperation can lead us to do almost anything. I unscrewed the cap, and just before I took a big dose, I noted something written in bold, bright red capital letters on the side of the bottle: *SHAKE WELL BEFORE USING*. I needed to shake the bottle well because the medicinal ingredients that would make me feel better had settled at the bottom of the bottle.

Life is like that. Proper priorities and personal perspectives have a way of settling on the bottom of the bottle while other lighter, less important things seem to rise to the top. So every once in a while God comes along and shakes us up. Why? Because He wants to use us. Days of spiritual recession when we are being shaken are actually not all bad for us. They rid us of excess baggage, get us back to the spiritual basics, and get our spiritual priorities back in order. So don't be surprised to realize that God has written *SHAKE WELL BEFORE USING* across the lives of His faithful.

34 FOOLISH PRESUMPTIONS

Come now, you who say, "Today or tomorrow we will go to such and such a city, spend a year there, buy and sell, and make a profit" . . . You boast in your arrogance. All such boasting is evil.

—JAMES 4:13, 16

The person James described in these verses lives as if tomorrow will never come. He is obsessed with making money. Materialism is his master. Motivated by greed, he is primarily concerned about accruing the world's wealth. He's not a bad guy. In fact, there's nothing to indicate he is either unethical or unprofessional. His ability to plan ahead serves him well, and he is self-confident, goal-oriented, and profit-motivated. And he lives life as a practical atheist with no consideration of God. Sadly, his "I can do it all on my own" philosophy reflects a common twenty-first-century mentality.

Still, most companies would hire someone like him. *Failure* was not in his vocabulary, and in his mind failing was an absolute impossibility. This man's attitude, not his actions, is the issue here. His problem was that he made all his plans without any consideration of God whatsoever. He lived by foolish presumptions. And James called him out: "You boast in your arrogance. All such boasting is evil."

First, in his arrogance, this man made presumptions about the *when*. He said, "Today or tomorrow." There's nothing wrong with planning ahead, but this man left out of his plans this key element: "If the Lord wills, we shall live and do this or that" (James 4:15). While he was boasting about what he might do tomorrow, James reminded him—and us—that life is but "a vapor that appears for a little time and then vanishes away" (James 4:14). The real problem is that we don't look far enough into the future and consider the eternal significance of how we're living now. James's warning is for any of us who make presumptions about tomorrow. God warned, "Do not boast about tomorrow, for you do not know what a day may bring forth" (Proverbs 27:1).

In his arrogance, this man also made presumptions about the *where*. He said he'd go "to such and such a city." Can you see this fellow in a strategy planning session with his team? Write-ups of all the research and data are scattered across the conference table. Population trends and growth potential of various locales are debated. Yet he drew his conclusions without any regard for the data, without any clue or concern that God's plans might be different from his own.

And our friend's foolish presumptions didn't stop here. He continued, this time making presumptions about the *what*. He said that he would "buy and sell, and make a profit." Now, there's nothing wrong with being goal-oriented unless we completely leave God out of our plans. Talk about someone driven by goals, consider Saul of Tarsus. He had his life all figured out—the when, the where, the what, and even the why: he was headed to Damascus to put down this Christian uprising (Acts 9). He thought he was doing God a service and that the Almighty would be pleased. However, God had other plans that Saul (soon to be called Paul) could not have even considered. God knocked Paul off his horse and transformed his life. For the rest of his days, Paul approached life with this addendum: "If it be the Lord's will, I will . . ."

Finally, in his arrogance, the man James described made presumptions about the *why,* the motivation for living as he was. His underlying motivation was to "make a profit." Again, there is nothing wrong with being profit-motivated. In fact, Jesus commended it (Matthew 25:14–30). This man's problem is that he still hadn't considered the will of the Lord in any of his planning. For many the chief end of life is to add a little more to the bottom line.

So what motivates you? There is nothing wrong with making a profit. But profits made without any desire to honor the Lord with our possessions often bring misery and mayhem, even heartbreak and heartache.

Our friend of whom James spoke complicated his predicament by arrogantly "boasting and bragging" about his plans. The warning for us is plain: don't make presumptions about the future without consulting God. This warning doesn't mean that we should be passive. We ought to do more detailed planning than anyone else. We should be goal-oriented and profit-motivated because we have Someone on our side guiding us and leading us, and He always knows best. He is also "able to do exceedingly abundantly above all that we ask or think" (Ephesians 3:20). And, as Christians, we need to include this in all our plans: "If the Lord wills" (James 4:15).

Perhaps you're experiencing your own recession of the soul, a period of reduced spiritual activity. Be watchful. Recessions—whether economic or spiritual—are often rooted in foolish presumptions.

JUST DO IT! Was James saying it's wrong to talk about the when, the where, the what, or the why? Not at all! In fact, as followers of Christ, we should be the best long-range, strategic planners around. We should know where we're headed and have an idea about how we're getting there. James's point was not about our actions; it was about our attitudes. Planning ahead is certainly not foolish, but planning ahead without including "If the Lord wills" is completely foolish. It is wise to set goals, but they will let us down if we leave God out of both formulating those goals and working to achieve them.

35   FORGOTTEN PERSPECTIVES

You do not know what will happen tomorrow. For what is your life? It is even a vapor that appears for a little time and then vanishes away.

—JAMES 4:14

*D*uring the Iraqi wars, our church sent thousands of New Testament Bibles with camouflage covers to American troops stationed in the Middle East. We heard from one young man who told of being in a desert bunker with artillery shells flying overhead. He took out one of these pocket Bibles, and it opened to James 4:14—"You do not know what will happen tomorrow. For what is your life? It is even a vapor that appears for a little time and then vanishes away." Many of us read this verse and pass right over it with little thought because of forgotten perspectives. If, like that young soldier, we were reading it while war was raging all around us, I am confident we might read it with a different perspective.

Too often and too easily, proper views of life and death are forgotten perspectives for many of us. Some people live as though this life is all there is. We even seek to camouflage the aging process and pretend it isn't happening. Death is just not a subject we want to dwell on. That's why many of us act and live as if we have a ninety-nine-year lease on our body with an option to renew. Death, however, is life's greatest certainty.

LIFE HAS ITS UNCERTAINTIES

James asked, "What is your life?" Secular scientists and philosophers have never been able to satisfactorily answer this question. As Christians, we know that life doesn't end when our physical bodies die. We know that we will go on living after death. In fact, God Himself has instilled within the soul of man a longing for life beyond this one. Even primitive people held this hope. The proof of this is found in cave drawings by people who lived thousands of years ago. And ancient Egyptians were buried in their tombs with eating utensils, weapons, and even servants, as proof of their belief that they would live again—somewhere. A thousand years from today you indeed will be alive—someplace.

James answered his own question "What is your life?" by saying that life "is even a vapor that appears for a little time and then vanishes away." A vapor is here one minute and gone the next. The steam arising from a teakettle on the stove appears for a moment and then vanishes.

The Bible uses many other metaphors to drive home the truth of the brevity of life. First Chronicles 29:15 reminds us that "our days on earth are as a shadow." Job put it like this: "My life is a breath" (Job 7:7) and "Now my days are swifter than a runner; they flee away" (9:25). David added, "My days are consumed like smoke" (Psalm 102:3).

The very moment we take our first breath, we begin to die. We all have an appointment with death awaiting us. As a pastor I have stood at the graves of those who met their death in wrecks and wars, by disease and decay. One way or another, if Jesus tarries, we will all die. No one knows when, but everyone knows it will happen.

James's point is that, for all of us, the length of life is uncertain. No matter how long we live, life is short. Addressing this uncertainty about the length of life, Solomon warned, "Do not boast about tomorrow, for you do not know what a day may bring forth" (Proverbs 27:1). And his father David added this:

> LORD, make me to know my end,
> And what is the measure of my days,
> That I may know how frail I am.
> Indeed, You have made my days as handbreadths,
> And my age is as nothing before You;
> Certainly every man at his best state is but vapor.
> Surely every man walks about like a shadow;
> Surely they busy themselves in vain;
> He heaps up riches,
> And does not know who will gather them.
>   (Psalm 39:4–6)

Yes, life has its uncertainties. Especially for those who live with forgotten perspectives.

LIFE HAS ITS CERTAINTIES

Life's greatest certainty is that it has an earthly end. It

"vanishes away." Our culture is busy trying to disguise the aging process. We color our hair, inject Botox around our eyes, and look for some miracle potion that will give us a few more years. Some people even go to the extreme and choose cryonics: they freeze their bodies after they die in hopes that some future medical breakthrough will provide a cure for their particular death-causing disease and enable them to live again.

But nothing will keep a single one of us from this ultimate appointment that is already on God's calendar. As the Bible says, "In Your book they all were written, the days fashioned for me, when as yet there were none of them" (Psalm 139:16).

When the late Peter Marshall was chaplain of the United States Senate, he often told a fable that illustrates the certainty of death. One day a wealthy merchant in Baghdad sent his servant to the market. Before long, the servant returned trembling and ashen-faced. He reported to his master, "I was down among the crowds in the marketplace and was jostled by someone in the crowd. When I turned around, I saw that Death had jostled me. She looked straight at me and made a threatening gesture. Please, Master, lend me your horse this night, that I might hurry to Samarra and hide there so Death cannot find me."

The merchant loaned his servant the swiftest horse, and he galloped away in haste. Later the merchant went to the marketplace and saw Death still standing there in the crowd. He went over to her and asked, "Why did you frighten my servant today and make a threatening gesture toward him?"

"Oh," replied Death. "That was not a threatening gesture at all. I was simply startled to see him here in Baghdad, for I have an appointment with him tonight in Samarra!"*

Yes, life has its certainties.

JUST DO IT! Each of us has our own appointment in Samarra. Don't allow foolish presumptions or forgotten perspectives to hide this fact from you or distract you. Furthermore, if you have placed your faith and trust in Jesus Christ, the One who holds "the keys of Hades and of Death" (Revelation 1:18), your appointment can mean rejoicing, not fear. Yet we all need to heed the call of Amos 4:12 that thunders down through the centuries: "Prepare to meet your God!"

John Doe, Disciple by Peter Marshall, copyright © 1963 by McGraw-Hill Book Company, Inc., first edition, pp 219–220.

FORSAKEN PRIORITIES

Instead you ought to say, "If the Lord wills, we shall live and do this or that." But now you boast in your arrogance. All such boasting is evil. Therefore, to him who knows to do good and does not do it, to him it is sin.

—JAMES 4:15–17

The story is told of a man riding his motorcycle along a winding country road. He stopped to talk with a preacher standing in the churchyard. The motorcyclist told the preacher he was on his way to town to sell his motorcycle. Paraphrasing James 4:15, the parson replied, "You ought to say, 'I am riding to town to sell my motorcycle . . . if it be the Lord's will.'" The man rolled his eyes, laughed out loud, and mocked the preacher's words. Then he roared off down the two-lane road sending up a cloud of gravel in his wake.

Late that afternoon the preacher was sitting on his front porch watching the sun go down. He looked down the long road and noticed a man stumbling and staggering from one side of the road to the other. As the preacher stood up for a better view, he noted that it was the same man with whom he had visited earlier in the day. The man's pants were torn to shreds, exposing his bruised and bloody knees. His right arm was in a makeshift sling. His shirt was half ripped off his back. His face was red and swollen, and one eye was completely shut. His hair was disheveled. His arms were scraped, and little pieces of gravel were embedded in them. Hurrying to his aid, the preacher inquired, "What happened?"

The man stammered, "After I left you, a big storm came out of nowhere. I tried to outrun it, but the rain pelted down upon me like lumps of lead. As I was going around a curve, I hit some loose gravel, and the motorcycle slid out from under me. I skidded a hundred feet on the pavement. I managed to get up, but the motorcycle was a total loss. Somehow I made my way to a nearby farmhouse. As I approached the door, a frightened woman pointed a shotgun in my face. I started running. She started shooting. And it started raining. I ran through the brush and briars. Finally, I came into a clearing and got under a tree to shield myself from the rain. As I stood there trying to pick the buckshot out of my backside, lightning struck the tree and knocked me out. When I came to, I started walking down this road."

The preacher then asked, "Well, where are you going now?"

The man replied, "I am going home"—and then he quickly added, "If it be the Lord's will!"

In today's passage, James was calling on us to get our priorities in order and to remember the bottom line when we make any and all our plans: "If it be the Lord's will." James was reminding us to not forsake God's will and God's way as we set our priorities.

GOD'S WILL

God does not veil His will from any of us who earnestly seek it. He wants us to not only know His will but to walk in it. Paul addressed this very point, saying, "[We] do not cease to pray for you, and to ask that you may be filled with the knowledge of His will in all wisdom and spiritual understanding" (Colossians 1:9).

True success in life is in finding God's will for our lives and then doing it—and according to that definition, few people have known the kind of success that the apostle Paul did. His driving motivation was to find God's will and do it, and he repeatedly said so. Upon leaving the believers in the church he planted in Ephesus, for instance, he said, "I will return again to you, God willing" (Acts 18:21). To those in the troubled church at Corinth, he wrote, "I will come to you shortly, if the Lord wills" (1 Corinthians 4:19). And to the church in Rome he wrote, "I make mention of you always in my prayers, making request if, by some means, now at last I may find a way in the will of God to come to you" (Romans 1:9–10). Paul was wise enough to know that all his plans should be made with the caveat "If the Lord wills."

To avoid spiritual recession we need to keep our priorities straight, and that means that God's desires should be our desires. The safest place in all the world is being in the middle of God's will for your life.

GOD'S WAY

Forsaken priorities come with straying from God's *way* in

our lives as well as His *will*, and James now raised a yellow warning flag: "To him who knows to do good and does not do it, to him it is sin." For the most part, when we hear the word *sin*, we think only of sins of commission—those willful, outward acts that violate God's law and love. But James was saying that our problem is not just doing what we shouldn't (sins of commission), but also in *not* doing what we should (sins of omission). Doing wrong is sin; *not* doing right is a sin as well. For example, just as it is a sin to tell an outright lie, it is also a sin to know the truth and not tell it.

If you miss rewards in heaven, it will not only be because of sins of commission but also sins of omission. And knowing the gospel but not embracing it is the most serious of all the sins of omission. Jesus said, "He who believes in Him is not condemned; but he who does not believe is condemned already, because he has not believed in the name of the only begotten Son of God" (John 3:18).

If you are numbered among those who think there will always be adequate time to get right with God, James was warning you. We are all only one heartbeat, one breath, away from eternity. Place your hand on your chest. Go ahead, do it. Feel your heart beating. It hasn't missed a beat since you were in your mother's womb. But at an already-appointed time, it will beat one last beat, followed by a final breath, and you will leave your body, the house you have lived in during this brief earthly journey. At that moment, what difference will it make if you have eaten vitamin-enriched foods, have acquired a lot of stuff, are buried in a mahogany casket, and are placed in a beautiful botanical garden—and then rise up in judgment to meet a God you don't know?

It's time to hear and heed James's inspired advice. Stop making foolish presumptions about tomorrow. To avoid the arrogance of our age, which results in our own spiritual recession, maintain a proper perspective on life and align your personal priorities with the Lord's. His will and His way are always best.

JUST DO IT! Forsaken priorities are the direct result of foolish presumptions. Now, I would never encourage anyone to get a body tattoo. However, I do challenge you to tattoo this phrase on your heart and mind: "If the Lord wills." In order to best determine God's will, be sure you know the Savior, be sure you know the Spirit, and be sure you know the Scripture. Trusting in Christ alone and knowing His gracious pardoning of your sin is the essential starting line. Then allow His Spirit within you to lead you according to His Word. God will never lead us to do anything contrary to what we find in Scripture. Also, as you meditate upon Scripture, you will often find His will for you right there in black and white. Then, just do it!

37   YOUR MONEY TALKS ... WHAT DOES IT SAY?

Come now, you rich, weep and howl for your miseries that are coming upon you! Your riches are corrupted, and your garments are moth-eaten. Your gold and silver are corroded, and their corrosion will be a witness against you and will eat your flesh like fire. You have heaped up treasure in the last days. Indeed the wages of the laborers who mowed your fields, which you kept back by fraud, cry out; and the cries of the reapers have reached the ears of the Lord of Sabaoth. You have lived on the earth in pleasure and luxury; you have fattened your hearts as in a day of slaughter. You have condemned, you have murdered the just; he does not resist you.

—JAMES 5:1–6

"Come now, you rich!" In other words, "Listen up, you rich people!" With these attention-grabbing words, James began the next paragraph of his letter—which many people simply skip over! They wrongly think it doesn't really apply to them. Instead, they think it's directed to those rich folks living behind the iron gates protecting their mansion— and they're glad the Lord is giving it to them!

Let me just say that I've seen two basic reactions to James 5:1–6. Some people without money sometimes feel they are a bit more spiritual than those who have it. Well, they aren't. On the other hand, some people with money somehow feel defensive, as though they have to apologize for having money. Well, they don't. These verses from James apply to every one of us, for being rich is relative. Compared with the overwhelming majority of the world's people, everyone reading this book is wealthy. Think about it. You probably own an automobile . . . with air conditioning, power windows, and power steering. Most of the world has never even sat in an automobile. You can afford a hamburger for lunch. Most of the world can't.

Over decades of ministry I have been privileged to preach around the world. I have been in the slums of Mumbai, journeyed through the African bush, sat with refugees in the Middle East, and been the dinner guest in the most remote and humble homes you can imagine. If those people were reading James 5 today, they would be thinking of people in America who make a minimum wage and are therefore wealthy.

The reality is, no matter how much money we may have, someone else has a lot more. No matter how little money we may have, someone else has far less. So we can be sure that James's words are directed to each one of us. No one is exempt. Wealth is, above all things, relative. I have known people without much money who were actually more preoccupied with possessing it than some who have large estates.

The real issue is not whether we have money, but whether our money has us! James was touching a sensitive nerve regarding the danger of materialism, the danger of being possessed and obsessed with stuff.

One problem in our affluent Western culture is that too many politicians—and too many individuals—think that most of our problems can be solved with money. So they raise taxes, redistribute the wealth, and create a dependent and entitled mentality in the process. Also, it seems the more money we have, the more money we think we need. The more we make, the more we spend. Too many salary raises have simply created more personal debt. Money is deceptive. Very subtly it can become the object of our worship. When we begin to possess significant amounts of money, it has a way of attempting to possess us.

That said, know that there is certainly no condemnation of wealth in these verses. Many of our heroes in the Bible were very wealthy individuals. Take Abraham: "Abram was very rich in livestock, in silver, and in gold" (Genesis 13:2). King David was certainly not in the welfare line himself: "He died in a good old age, full of days and riches and honor" (1 Chronicles 29:28). And his son Solomon accumulated more than Abraham and David put together. Joseph of Arimathaea, in whose tomb Jesus was laid, is identified as a "rich man" (Matthew 27:57). And Barnabas, the wealthy landowner, made possible the expansion of the early church when he sold a valuable piece of real estate on the island of Cyprus and gave the money to the apostles (Acts 4:36–37).

So if there is nothing wrong with wealth in and of itself, then why these words of warning from James? As he will explain, the real issue with wealth is not in having it, but in how we *get* it, how we *guard* it, and how we *give* it.

The way we handle our money can bring—to use James's words—"miseries" upon us. The underlying idea of the word conveys that money may bring joy temporarily, but that joy is followed by misery. If our money is accumulated by ungodly means, it will bring misery sooner or later. It always does. If we hoard our wealth, it does no good for anyone, and we will be of all men most miserable in the end. Also, if we simply give our money to all types of self-indulgence, the result is also misery.

Don't misunderstand James here. The point he was making is that how we get money, how we guard it, and how we give it will reveal what is truly in our hearts.

JUST DO IT! Your money talks. In fact, it speaks volumes about what you think is important in life. It is so much a reflection of what is inside us that Jesus spoke often about it. In one out of every three of His sermons, He spoke about money. He told thirty-eight parables, and one-third of them deal with us and our possessions.

One of Jesus' most poignant statements is, "Where your treasure is, there your heart will be also"

(Matthew 6:21). Jesus knew your treasure would not follow your heart, but that your heart would follow where you put your money. Thus, there is a real possibility that the accountant who prepares your annual income tax returns knows more about your spiritual condition than your pastor or even your prayer partner. Yes, "where your treasure is, there your heart will be also." So be careful about how you get your money, how you guard it, and how you give it.

38   How We Get It

Come now, you rich, weep and howl for your miseries that are coming upon you! . . . The wages of the laborers who mowed your fields, which you kept back by fraud, cry out; and the cries of the reapers have reached the ears of the Lord of Sabaoth . . . You have condemned, you have murdered the just; he does not resist you.

—JAMES 5:1, 4, 6

The issue of how we get our wealth is vitally important to God, and that thought pervades the first paragraph of James 5. As he wrote these words to the scattered church, James had in mind a man who received his money through two particular means: exploitation and expropriation.

James began with an accusation of *exploitation*. He was not speaking softly here: "The wages of the laborers who mowed your field, which you kept back by fraud, *cry out;* and . . . have reached the ears of the Lord" (emphasis added). Never does the Bible condemn the acquisition of wealth by legal and legitimate means. James was calling out those who acquired their wealth through illegal or illegitimate means. A man who had contracted to pay his employees a certain amount exploited them by refusing to pay them what was owed. James called it what it was: fraud. From the start, the landowner never intended to pay the workers what he had promised them for their services. There are still those around today who are looking for any and every loophole in agreements that can be found. But, as James warned, God, the righteous Judge, is listening and looking.

Throughout its pages the Bible gives clear and cautious warning against acquiring wealth through exploitative means. In Leviticus 19:13, we read, "You shall not cheat your neighbor, nor rob him. The wages of him who is hired shall not remain with you all night until morning." Deuteronomy 24:14–15 brings us this warning: "You shall not oppress a hired servant who is poor and needy, whether one of your brethren or one of the aliens who is in your land within your gates. Each day you shall give him his wages, and not let the sun go down on it, for he is poor and has set his heart on it; lest he cry out against you to the Lord, and it be sin to you." God heard the prayers of the Jewish slaves in Egypt: "The children of Israel groaned because of the bondage, and they cried out; and their cry came up to God because of the bondage" (Exodus 2:23). Jesus added bluntly, "The laborer is worthy of his wages" (Luke 10:7).

There is an interesting message hidden behind the verb tenses found in James 5:4. The verb translated *mowed* is in the aorist tense, which indicates the task was done at a point in time: the job had been accomplished; the task, finished. The work was done. No argument here. When we read that this landowner failed to pay, we find it in the imperfect tense, meaning that the employer had held back the pay and had no intention of paying it. Then, when James said these wages "cry out," he formed it in the present tense: they were continuously crying out about this injustice. In life, payday comes sooner or later. Especially when God is looking and listening.

Next comes a stinging accusation from the pen of James: "You have condemned, you have murdered the just; he does not resist you." Now we see that this man is guilty not only of exploitation but of *expropriation* as well. In accusing this man of "condemning" his workers, James borrowed a judicial term for the manner in which the rich pervert the legal system to accumulate wealth. The term implies that some people control and manipulate the courts so much that justice is eliminated. In other words, their money buys them power to use the courts to take away someone else's means of support. This landowner thought he had the power to control the system and so prevent his workers from opposing him. As he deprived them of what was theirs, it was as if he murdered them.

There are ways of killing people without actually taking their physical lives. We can kill a person's reputation by vicious and untruthful slander. We can kill a person's incentive and drive with constant criticism and rebukes. Here James was pointing out a man who would stop at nothing to gain a little more for himself.

Victims of crimes don't stand up against injustice when those with financial means—and therefore power—control the system, rendering the victims unable to defend themselves. Earlier in his letter James had commented on this very point: "You have dishonored the poor man. Do not the rich oppress you and drag you into the courts?" (James 2:6). James wanted people to know that, in the end, wealth gained by any illegitimate means brings nothing more than "miseries."

It was the love of money that was at the root of Jesus' own betrayal. Judas was the treasurer of the group. He managed the money. He loved it. In fact, he sold the Lord out for thirty measly pieces of silver. And look at how "he got it." In the end, he epitomizes someone whose final scene is "misery." Yes, money talks. What is how you got your money saying about you? If you don't get money in the right way, sooner or later your gold and silver will "cry out" against you.

JUST DO IT! Remember, *rich* is a relative term. No matter how much you have, someone else has more. No matter how little you have, someone else has less. James's message, with its warning, is for every one of us.

Consider this. Your employer is paying you for an eight-hour day, but are you actually working only seven of them? Perhaps you take a little extra time for lunch, or maybe an additional afternoon break. Do you ever sit at your desk playing a computer game or reading something unrelated to your work? If you are doing any of these, you are stealing from your employer. You might as well sneak into the petty cash drawer and help yourself to a little bit of the cash!

Believers in the workforce ought to be the most conscientious and diligent workers in the office, for they are doing their work "as to the Lord" (Ephesians 6:5–8). Ill-gotten gains will come back to haunt us. Your money talks. What does it say about you?

39   How We Guard It

Come now, you rich, weep and howl for your miseries that are coming upon you! Your riches are corrupted, and your garments are moth-eaten. Your gold and silver are corroded, and their corrosion will be a witness against you and will eat your flesh like fire. You have heaped up treasure in the last days.

—JAMES 5:1–3

It's not just how we get our money, but also how we guard it that James confronted. His point of interest here is hoarded wealth, riches that are "heaped up" in the last days. We actually get our word *thesaurus* from this phrase. Meaning "a collection," this word carries with it the connotation of getting all we can and storing it up. This is not an attack on wisely having a savings account. In fact, the Bible places its stamp of approval on our fiscal responsibility. When Paul was informing the Corinthians of a future visit, he wrote saying, "I will not be burdensome to you; for I do not seek yours, but you. For the children ought not to lay up for the parents, but the parents for the children" (2 Corinthians 12:14). He commended parents for saving money for their children's future needs.

At issue here is hoarded wealth that is either owed to others

or that could be used to spread the gospel "in the last days." In James's mind, to hoard wealth is deceitful, decadent, and deceptive.

HOARDED WEALTH IS DECEITFUL

Guarded wealth promises joy but does not deliver. When we begin to make money a god, it ceases to bless us and begins to be a curse. It seems that the more money we have, the more we want, thinking that money will ultimately bring happiness. But that is a lie.

Jesus was hitting hard at this point with His parable of the rich fool. It is the perfect illustration of the deceitfulness of guarded, hoarded wealth:

The ground of a certain rich man yielded plentifully. And he thought within himself, saying, "What shall I do, since I have no room to store my crops?" So he said, "I will do this: I will pull down my barns and build greater, and there I will store all my crops and my goods. And I will say to my soul, 'Soul, you have many goods laid up for many years; take your ease; eat, drink, and be merry.'" But God said to him, "Fool! This night your soul will be required of you; then whose will those things be which you have provided?" (Luke 12:16–20).

Jesus then said, "So is he who lays up treasure for himself, and is not rich toward God" (Luke 12:21). Hoarded wealth is deceitful: it gives us the illusion of security for the future. Suddenly this rich man had no future on this earth.

So money will not bring happiness, nor does it guarantee a long future. Yet money plays the good role in our life of

enabling us to have things we need. It is far better, though, to have in life the things money *cannot* buy.

I have a small diamond stickpin I once wore on my ties. The diamond wasn't always on a stickpin. It was first in the wedding ring I gave my wife in 1970. We were students in those days, and all I could afford was a ring with one small diamond. In fact, if you examine the diamond closely, you can easily see a large carbon chip in the middle of it. I would be ashamed to tell you how little I paid for that ring. However, symbolized by that ring was a world of love and the confidence that God had brought us together and had a plan for our lives. Around the same time a college friend gave his fiancée one of the largest and most beautiful diamond rings I had ever seen. It was worth several thousands of dollars. Sadly, their marriage did not last two years.

Money may buy million-dollar houses, but it can't transform them into homes. Sometimes the most miserable people in the world live behind those big iron gates and carved mahogany doors. What really matters most in life is not what your money can buy, but what it can't buy. Wealth that is simply "heaped up" is deceitful: it will not satisfy.

HOARDED WEALTH IS DECADENT

Money can also be decadent when hoarded. It decays. If we don't use it, we ultimately lose it. At best, the money we earn and spend and save is temporal. Only the riches we deposit in the bank of heaven have eternal value. That's why Jesus warned, "Do not lay up for yourselves treasures on earth,

where moth and rust destroy and where thieves break in and steal; but lay up for yourselves treasures in heaven, where neither moth nor rust destroys and where thieves do not break in and steal" (Matthew 6:19–20).

With these words of our Lord in mind, James said, "Your riches are corrupted, and your garments are moth-eaten. Your gold and silver are corroded." James was so certain of the temporary and decaying nature of riches that he described the decay as if it had already happened. In the first-century world, there were no banks, no certificates of deposit, no mutual funds, no stocks or bonds or other investment vehicles. A man's wealth was measured in grain, garments, or gold. Remember, the rich fool in Jesus' story built more barns to store his grain harvests. But grain "corrupts" or "rots" (as some translations say) when it sits there rather than being used.

Garments in the ancient world were also symbols of wealth. Joseph blessed his brothers with garments as gifts when they were reunited in Egypt (Genesis 45:22). It was the desire for an expensive Babylonian robe that led to Achan's downfall after Jericho's fall (Joshua 7:10–26). Naaman brought Elisha garments as gifts (2 Kings 5:23). James said that hoarded garments, used as ancient savings accounts, would eventually become "moth-eaten."

Unfortunately, I have had my own personal experience with moths. I once had a nice winter coat in the back of my closet that they destroyed. A moth is subtle and silent, lurking behind the scenes. It is not like other insects. A roach will *badger* and taunt you, eating away at cabinets and leaving droppings on drain boards. Crickets will *bug* you (no pun intended). They make noise but can't be found. A mosquito will *bite* you. A fly will *bother* you. But a moth? It will *beguile* you. It keeps to itself. It will not bug you, or bite you, or bother you. It is quiet as it hangs out in the back of your closet and does its work in secret. Garments, like grain, become ruined when they aren't used.

And then there is gold. Lack of use causes metals to decay and corrode. A hinge on a gate that hasn't been opened in months will rust and corrode. However, as most of us know, real gold will not rust. James was indicating that our wealth is really just fool's gold: it has no eternal value. It is quite a shock to find out that what we thought would bring us happiness doesn't deliver. James's point is that hoarded wealth that isn't used is both deceitful and decaying.

HOARDED WEALTH IS DECEPTIVE

As we mentioned earlier, wealth brings with it a false sense of security about the future. The stock market, for instance, is up one day, down the next. Riches are uncertain. James's contemporaries experienced the deceptiveness of wealth firsthand. Within a few years of writing this letter, Jerusalem was completely destroyed by the Romans, and all the accumulated wealth of the Jews—their security blanket for the future— was taken from them.

It's deceptive to think our security is found in hoarded wealth. In fact, James warned that it will one day "witness against you." When you stand before the judgment seat of

Christ, the question will not be, "How much did you make?" More likely the question will be, "What did you do with what you had?" Your money will speak that day: it will either witness for you or against you.

What a tragedy to come to the end of life and have treasure laid up for this world only. We came into this world naked, without anything. We will leave it the same way. We can't take a single material thing with us. We tend to forget this truth, but we don't even own our possessions. Everything belongs to God. We are only stewards. We are simply passing through.

Hoarded wealth is deceitful. It is decaying. And it is, above all things, deceptive.

JUST DO IT! At some point after your death, a few family members and maybe a couple of friends will gather in a lawyer's office to read your last will and testament. Your will is your last chance to give a testimony about what you think is most important in this life. Yes, on that day your money will be talking loud and clear. What will it say about the importance you placed in the gospel of Jesus Christ?

40   How We Give It

You have lived on the earth in pleasure and luxury; you have fattened your hearts as in a day of slaughter.

—JAMES 5:5

*O*ur money speaks loudest when it comes to how we give it. Some individuals give large amounts . . . to themselves in self-indulgence. And this is the individual James had in mind when he issued this accusation: "You have lived on the earth in pleasure and luxury."

James's words get harsher: "You have fattened your hearts as in a day of slaughter." I relate well to this imagery, having grown up in Fort Worth, known for the stockyards that once marked the beginning of the Chisholm Trail. To this day, out on the North Side, you can walk the streets and see (and smell) those stockyards. The cattle in those pens are fed the finest of grains to fatten them up. Little do they realize they are going to be slaughtered. So they eat and eat and eat, enjoying the pleasures of the moment. The more they eat, the sooner they will be led to the slaughterhouse. When they get good and fat, the attendants throw a little corn in front of those mindless cows. Continuing in their self-indulgent ways, they follow the corn trail right out of their pen and right into the shoot—to the slaughterhouse next door.

James was saying that some people are just like those Texas cattle. They keep fattening themselves up, never realizing they are hastening the day of their own demise. They are headed to their own day of reckoning. Yet, as they follow their own self-indulgent appetite, they become too blind to see where it is taking them.

One day each of us will stand before our Maker. I doubt He will ask to see whether your Bible is all marked up and underlined. And I don't think He will want to see your diary or prayer journal that contains your innermost secrets and prayer requests. Some of us may be shocked to learn the most telling sign of what is most important to us in this life will be our checkbooks. Our cancelled checks and ATM debits say a lot about where our heart really is. Money talks. And how we use money speaks volumes about what we truly deem important.

Since how we use money is important to God, He has provided some laws to govern our giving and the stewardship of our possessions. First is the law of *clarification:* God owns all the wealth in this world and in the world to come. Everything belongs to Him. He owns "the cattle on a thousand hills" (Psalm 50:10). In David's words, "All that is in heaven and in earth is Yours" (1 Chronicles 29:11). And in the Psalms he added, "The earth is the Lord's, and all its fullness" (Psalm 24:1). Every single thing belongs to God, including what is in my bank account and stock portfolio—and in yours as well.

Next comes the law of *circulation*: God wants His wealth in circulation. In the beginning the theme of God's economy was simple: give, give, give. The sun gave. The earth gave. The animals gave. Man gave. But Satan slithered into our lives and introduced a new concept: get, get, get. We became greedy and began to live by our enemy's philosophy. But this was never God's plan.

The laws of *clarification* and *circulation* are followed by the law of *cooperation*: all of God's wealth will one day belong to His children, His heirs. The problem is that too many of us are hoarding wealth and not cooperating with His plan to give. At this point as Paul said, we are "heirs of God and joint heirs with Christ" (Romans 8:17). This is an awesome reality. We are not equal heirs with Christ but "joint heirs" with Him. God owns all the wealth in this world. And all His wealth belongs to His heirs.

This brings us to the law of *cultivation*. The way to appropriate God's wealth is to give. One of the most well-known biblical principles is that we never reap until we sow. Jesus said, "Give, and it will be given to you: good measure, pressed down, shaken together, and running over will be put into your bosom. For with the same measure that you use, it will be measured back to you" (Luke 6:38). To quote King David, "We can give out of God's hand." Put differently, we give out of His unlimited resources, actually giving from His hand to others. King David said it best: "For all things come from You, and of Your own [hand] we have given You" (1 Chronicles 29:14).

To recap, God owns all the wealth in the world, He wants it in circulation, and it will one day belong to us, who are joint heirs with Christ. The way we are to appropriate God's riches is to give, and that is very countercultural. We live in a world where accumulation is the name of the game. But one day we will answer for what we did with what God gave us along this life journey.

The fundamental danger with accumulated wealth is that it has a way of keeping our focus on this world. Too often, once we begin to possess wealth, it has a devious way of beginning to possess us. We must get our money honestly, guard it loosely, and give it generously to Christ's causes.

JUST DO IT! The Bible says, "Do not be deceived, God is not mocked; for whatever a man sows, that he will also reap" (Galatians 6:7). Paul set forth the universal law of the harvest here: you reap *what* you sow. If you plant corn, you are not going to reap wheat. You will reap what you sow in life as well. Do not be deceived at this point. When you give to God, He has His own supernatural way of giving back to you.

You reap *after* you sow. Some people wonder why their harvest never comes in life. They wait. They hope. But if they haven't sown and planted the seed, they will never gather a harvest. By God's design, you give to get, but only so that you can give again.

Finally, you reap *more* than you sow. If you plant a single grain of corn, you will reap a cornstalk with hundreds of other grains like itself. It works. Try it. It's God's way.

Your money talks: how you *get* it, how you *guard* it, and how you *give* it speak volumes about your values and priorities.

41   Apocalypse Now?

Therefore be patient, brethren, until the coming of the Lord. See how the farmer waits for the precious fruit of the earth, waiting patiently for it until it receives the early and latter rain. You also be patient. Establish your hearts, for the coming of the Lord is at hand. Do not grumble against one another, brethren, lest you be condemned. Behold, the Judge is standing at the door! My brethren, take the prophets, who spoke in the name of the Lord, as an example of suffering and patience. Indeed we count them blessed who endure. You have heard of the perseverance of Job and seen the end intended by the Lord—that the Lord is very compassionate and merciful. But above all, my brethren, do not swear, either by heaven or by earth or with any other oath. But let your "Yes" be "Yes," and your "No," "No," lest you fall into judgment.

—JAMES 5:7–12

"Be patient . . . until the coming of the Lord." With these words James directed our attention to the last days. There are a lot of prophets of doom around today who try to fit every world event into some type of prophetic Scripture. If we listened to these voices, we'd live in panic and fear, and our garages and storage units would be filled to the top with freeze-dried foods as we awaited Armageddon. Yet, into the world's chaos James said, "Be patient . . . until the coming of the Lord."

As I typed these words, my mind flashed back to my grandmother's lap and an old worn-out book about a critter named Chicken Little. Aptly named, Chicken Little was minding his own business, scratching in the dirt under a tree, when an acorn fell and hit him. He began to shout, "The sky is falling! The sky is falling! I am going to rush to tell the king." Along the way, he met a hen and shared his story. The hen decided to accompany Chicken Little on his journey.

On the way, they met a rooster. The hen told the rooster, "The sky is falling!" When the rooster asked how she knew this, she said she'd heard it from Chicken Little, who then chimed in, "Yes, I saw it with my own eyes and heard it with my own ears, and a piece of it hit me when it fell." So the rooster joined the entourage, and soon they came upon a duck, then a goose, and, later, a turkey—and all joined in the march to the king.

When the group met up with a fox, Chicken Little went through his whole story. Then the sly fox said, "Let's go into my den, and I will tell the king." And the last line of that little book was cemented in my mind: "So they all ran into Foxy Loxy's den, and the king was never told that the sky was falling."

Today, every major world crisis prompts someone else to say, "The sky is falling! Armageddon is on the way!" Sadly, these cries divert our attention from appropriating all the

blessings of Christ's first coming. We become focused on His Second Coming thanks to those who keep shouting, "The sky is falling!"

The beautiful good news is that our Lord will, indeed, make another visit to planet Earth. His Second Coming will be the greatest event in all of human history, and it could happen before you finish reading this chapter. The Jesus who came the first time as a Suffering Servant will come again as the King of kings and the Lord of lords.

Let's learn more about this moment.

WHAT is the Lord's coming? It is the fulfillment of His promise to "come again and receive you to Myself" (John 14:3). Jesus Christ is coming again to planet Earth in bodily form. His presence will be with us. He will invade this world, conquer evil, and usher in an age of peace.

WHOSE coming is it? It is the Lord's coming. Two thousand years ago, as He ascended from the Mount of Olives back to the Father, the angelic messenger said, "This same Jesus, who was taken up from you into heaven, will so come in like manner as you saw Him go into heaven" (Acts 1:11). The last promise in the Bible comes from the lips of our Lord: "Surely I am coming quickly" (Revelation 22:20). And it is immediately followed by the last prayer in the Bible: "Even so, come, Lord Jesus" (v. 20)!

WHY is Jesus coming back? As prophesied in Isaiah 53, His first coming was as the Suffering Servant who died on the cross for your sins and mine. Jesus will return as victor over sin and death to execute judgment. He will separate the

wheat from the chaff and the sheep from the goats, and He will usher in a time of peace on earth and an eternity in His presence. As James said, "The Judge is standing at the door!"

WHERE is He coming? He will come first "in the air." Paul said, "The Lord Himself will descend from heaven with a shout, with the voice of an archangel, and with the trumpet of God. And the dead in Christ will rise first. Then we who are alive and remain shall be caught up together with them in the clouds to meet the Lord in the air. And thus we shall always be with the Lord" (1 Thessalonians 4:16–17). First, Jesus will come *for* us; then He will come *with* us. When He comes back to the earth, "in that day His feet will stand on the Mount of Olives, which faces Jerusalem on the east. And the Mount of Olives shall be split in two" (Zechariah 14:4).

A final important question is WHEN is He coming? Some of Jesus' followers say His return is imminent. Perhaps it will be very soon—but perhaps not. No one knows. One time, when asked about the when, Jesus replied, "Of that day and hour no one knows, not even the angels of heaven, but My Father only" (Matthew 24:36). We should live each day as if Christ could return at any moment. It would surely make a difference in what we do, what we say, and where we go, wouldn't it?

We should look expectantly toward this great day of our Lord's coming without running after every so-called prophet who cries, "The sky is falling." Our forefathers in the first generations of the church lived daily with the hope of His return. They greeted each other saying, "Maranatha!" ("The

Lord is coming"). They got up each morning to live the day as if it were their last opportunity to live for Christ before He returned.

We should live as if Christ died yesterday and the cross is still standing tall atop Golgotha. We should also live as if Christ rose this morning and we can still see His grave clothes, folded neatly, inside the empty tomb. And we should live as if He is coming back tomorrow. And, always, "[being] patient . . . until the Lord's coming."

JUST DO IT! The Bible speaks of the coming of Christ, born of a virgin in an obscure Middle Eastern village, fulfilling centuries-old prophecies. The Bible speaks of the coming of the Holy Spirit, foretold by the prophet Joel and fulfilled on the Day of Pentecost when the Holy Spirit came to indwell the believer, never to leave us, empowering us to serve our God. The Bible also speaks of a major coming yet to be fulfilled, and that is the Second Coming of the Lord Jesus Christ to planet Earth. This future coming will be the climax of human history and the fulfillment of the Lord's last promise in all the Bible: "I am coming quickly" (Revelation 22:20). Be patient until He comes!

42   Look Up . . . Be Calm

Therefore be patient, brethren, until the coming of the Lord. See how the farmer waits for the precious fruit of the earth, waiting patiently for it until it receives the early and latter rain.

—JAMES 5:7

Speculations and apocalyptic predictions of Christ's Second Coming are certainly nothing new. They were occurring thirty years after His resurrection and ascension. James was attempting to counter such predictions with his admonition to "be patient." The word describes a distance runner who focuses on the last lap as he runs his race. James was saying, "Don't let stumbling or fear get you off track. Look up to the Lord and stay calm."

The believers to whom James was writing had expected the Lord to have already returned, so they were anxious about the Second Coming of Christ and becoming more and more impatient. Furthermore, these believers were experiencing tremendous persecution by the Romans. Thus, James was calling for patience—and courage and calm—in the face of these adverse circumstances.

He encouraged these believers to remain patient until the Lord's coming, and you and I are still living in the great

"until," awaiting this climactic event. Any woman who has birthed a child can identify with this admonition to wait. As excited as a pregnant woman may be, the only thing she can do is be patient "until" the baby arrives.

And with historians telling us that James was most likely a farmer in his earlier years, it's not surprising that he likens our patiently waiting on the Lord's return to a farmer waiting for the harvest. He said, "See how the farmer waits for the precious fruit of the earth, waiting patiently for it until it receives the early and latter rain."

Farmers everywhere know the feeling of planting their crops and then waiting for them to come in. In Israel, for example, farmers plow and plant their crops in the autumn months. So the autumn rains are necessary to keep the earth soft and to help the seeds germinate. Then the crop depends on the spring showers to help it mature. The autumn and spring rains—the "early and latter rain"—are beyond the farmer's control. He is totally dependent on the Lord. He waits patiently, for the harvest—that comes in late spring—is well worth the wait.

Think now about the period after the seeds are planted when there is no visible evidence that anything is growing. The wise farmer knows there is nothing he can do to accelerate the harvest. So, knowing that God is at work underground in the process, the farmer waits patiently—but he works as he waits: cultivating, watering, cutting away weeds. The same is true with those of us who know and love Christ. We cannot hurry His return, and while we wait, we work. We plant the seeds, cultivate the ground, fertilize, and care for the crops in anticipation of the coming harvest.

Waiting periods in farming—and in life—are not without testings and trials. Sometimes the weather is too hot; other times, too cold. An overabundance of rain can cause a crop to rot; a drought can cause the crop to scorch and wither. Hailstorms can strip the fruit off the stalks. If a freeze comes too early, the crop can die. And all a farmer can do is stay calm and trust the Lord to bring in the harvest.

Clearly, James was telling us that, as believers, we should await the Lord's coming in the same way a farmer awaits his harvest: by looking up and remaining calm. A farmer can't control the weather, and we can't control Christ's return.

As we wait, we will certainly encounter times of testing and trials as well as those people who wring their hands and panic, fearful of an imminent world holocaust.

The farmer is a wise teacher. Learn from him. Look up to the Lord and be calm. "Be patient . . . until the coming of the Lord."

JUST DO IT! Current world events— all of which are beyond our control—may have us wringing our hands and worrying about the future of our children and grandchildren. For what it's worth, when I look back over my life, 90 percent of the things I worried about never even happened.

Worrying is like rocking in a rocking chair. It may give you something to do, but it will never get you anywhere. Stop looking around at all the atrocities and the resulting or potential problems. Start looking up to the Lord and be calm. Jesus is coming—on His own timetable—and He will be right on time!

43 LOOK IN ... BE CLEAN

You also be patient. Establish your hearts, for the coming of the Lord is at hand. Do not grumble against one another, brethren, lest you be condemned. Behold, the Judge is standing at the door!
—JAMES 5:8–9

When we find ourselves in a holding pattern—in this case, waiting for the Lord to return—it's easy to become irritated and frustrated, to hold grudges and to "grumble against one another." There is potential within each of us to be bitter and resentful. Thus James turned our attention from looking up to looking in: "Establish your hearts, for the coming of the Lord is at hand." Since Christ could return any day and at any time, then we should keep our hearts clean, and be ready to meet Him at any moment.

"Establishing your heart" is something only you can do. No one can do it for you. As the voice and tense of this phrase indicate, the subject has to take action. It is not my brother or my sister or anyone else. I am responsible for me. Until the Lord returns, therefore, we should not just look up to Him and be calm. We should also look in and be clean. We should establish our hearts.

James called upon us to cease grumbling against one

another. This refers to resentment buried deep within our hearts that manifests itself in negative and sometimes harsh words. James essentially said, "Stop grumbling! Don't do it." Why? Because "the Judge is standing at the door." Jesus used this same imagery: "Behold, I stand at the door and knock. If anyone hears My voice and opens the door, I will come in to him and dine with him, and he with Me" (Revelation 3:20). Jesus stands at the door of our hearts. We may be fooling others with our hypocrisy, but we are not fooling this righteous Judge who keeps watch at the door of our hearts. And this Judge knows the secrets of every heart.

In this chapter James emphasized the Lord's coming, but is there any hard evidence that truly points to this event? The Bible foretells that certain things will happen before Jesus' coming, and perhaps the two most significant of those happenings have taken place in my own lifetime. The first of these has to do with a *particular place,* specifically a small sliver of real estate between the Jordan River to the east and the Mediterranean Sea to the west, about the size of the tiny state of New Jersey. Today we know it as the nation of Israel. God promised that, before Christ returns, Israel would be reestablished as a nation and become a major player on the world scene. God said, "I will bring back the captives of My people Israel; they shall build the waste cities and inhabit them; they shall plant vineyards and drink wine from them; they shall also make gardens and eat fruit from them. I will plant them in their land, and no longer shall they be pulled up from the land I have given them" (Amos 9:14–15). My generation has seen both the miraculous rebirth of the state of Israel and its remarkable rise to prominence as a world power. For the first time since the Babylonian captivity (586–538 BC), the Jews are ruling their own country from their capital city of Jerusalem. After twenty-five hundred years in exile, the Jews are back in their Holy Land and in their Holy City. And many of us have witnessed this development with our own eyes.

This particular place of Israel is the site of another significant sign of Jesus' return, and that sign is a *peculiar people,* with *peculiar* meaning "belonging to someone"; in this case, belonging to God. After the forty years of wilderness wanderings, Moses stood at Nebo and preached a prophetic message before his people crossed the Jordan and journeyed into the promised land. Moses said, "The Lord will scatter you among the peoples, and you will be left few in number among the nations where the Lord will drive you" (Deuteronomy 4:27). But Ezekiel talked to the Jews about a day when God would "take you from among the nations, gather you out of all countries, and bring you into your own land" (Ezekiel 36:24). From all over the world, these peculiar people have returned to their ancient homeland, revived the Hebrew language, and reestablished their Hebrew state—all in fulfillment of Bible prophecy.

Clearly, such ample evidence of the last days should motivate us not only to look up to God and be calm as we await Jesus' return, but also to look in and make sure we are clean and ready to meet Him on that day. Nearly two thousand years have elapsed since James penned these words, and the Judge who is at the door has not stepped across the threshold—*yet*. However, we must remember that God is not operating on Central Standard Time. He is on His own schedule, and He will be absolutely right on time, not a minute early and not a minute late. Until then, it is imperative that we believers "establish our hearts"—that we look in and are clean.

JUST DO IT! So how do we keep our hearts clean? First John 1:7 says, "If we walk in the light as He is in the light, we have fellowship with one another, and the blood of Jesus Christ His Son cleanses us from all sin." Note *sin* is in the singular here: it refers to our inherent sin nature that we deal with when we recognize ourselves as sinners, acknowledge Jesus as God's Son, and welcome Him as our Savior and Lord. At this point of being born again, Christ's shed blood "cleanses us from all sin."

First John 1:9 says, "If we confess our sins, He is faithful and just to forgive us our sins and to cleanse us from all unrighteousness." Note *sins* is plural here, indicating that just because we come to Christ doesn't mean we cease sinning. It means that we are able to go to Him, confess our sins daily, and receive His forgiveness. Although our sin was covered and paid for by Jesus' body on the cross, and we received forgiveness and salvation by trusting in Christ, we need to *daily* confess and forsake our personal *daily* sins in *daily* prayer. When we confess our sins, we establish our hearts.

Look in—and be clean—until the coming of the Lord.

44   LOOK BACK . . . BE CHALLENGED

My brethren, take the prophets, who spoke in the name of the Lord, as an example of suffering and patience. Indeed we count them blessed who endure. You have heard of the perseverance of Job and seen the end intended by the Lord—that the Lord is very compassionate and merciful.

—JAMES 5:10–11

*H*aving called upon his hearers to look up and to look in, James next challenged us to look back to those who have gone before us. James called upon believers to "take the prophets," to consider their example and learn from them. When they were put in holding patterns, they were tempted to give up. But they are examples of patience to us today. These prophets were not just looking toward the first coming of the Lord for their own benefit; they were also pointing their hearers in that direction. In fact, no one endured more suffering and persecution than they did as they awaited Jesus' coming.

Jesus referred to these suffering prophets near the end of His earthly life when He was viewing Jerusalem from the Mount of Olives. He cried, "O Jerusalem, Jerusalem, the one who kills the prophets and stones those who are sent to her! How often I wanted to gather your children together, as a hen gathers her chicks under her wings, but you were not willing!" (Matthew 23:37). And hear some of Stephen's last words as he was stoned outside Jerusalem's Lion's Gate: "Which of the prophets did your fathers not persecute? And they killed those who foretold the coming of the Just One, of whom you now have become the betrayers and murderers" (Acts 7:52).

Being aware of both the patience of the prophets and the price they paid for their faith challenges me in this day of grace to keep moving forward in my own faith. This time of waiting and being encouraged by those who have waited before me builds up my anticipation for Jesus' return.

Looking back enriches my waiting just as it can enrich other aspects of life. I once attended a graduation ceremony at West Point. The long history and tradition—the buildup—at that military academy was rich and distinctive. Similarly, anyone who ever walked out into center field at the old Yankee Stadium to view the statues of such greats as Babe Ruth and Lou Gehrig knows how tradition—or buildup—enriches a sport.

History and tradition are even more important in our Christian experience. Thus, James reminded us to look back and be challenged by those who went before us as we ourselves await the Lord's coming. Look back at Hosea: his marriage failed, but he hung in (Hosea 3:1–3). Look back at Daniel: he was thrown into a lions' den for standing firm in his faith, but God delivered him (Daniel 6:1–28). Look back at Jeremiah: he was arrested, accused of being a traitor, and thrown into a well to die (Jeremiah 37–38). But he looked up, and God delivered him.

And then there's the roll call of the faithful—of persecuted prophets among them—listed in Hebrews 11! Those of us who have been rejected by family members can look back to Abel (v. 4). Those who are misunderstood can look back to Noah (v. 7). Those battling with a crisis of faith and who seem to be up against the impossible can look back to Abraham (vv. 8–10). If you've been used or abused, look back to Joseph (v. 22). Those of us confronted with seemingly insurmountable obstacles in life can look back to Joshua (v. 30). And those seeking to move beyond a sinful past can look back to Rahab (v. 31). James was saying, "Look back and be challenged."

Next, James called us to turn our attention from the persecution of the prophets to the perseverance of Job. Now, if you think you have problems, take a look at the Old Testament book of Job. Everything seemed to be against him. He lost his wealth. He lost his health. His friends turned on him. And, as if that weren't enough, his own wife looked him in the face and said, "Curse God and die!" (Job 2:9). For a while Job may have felt as if even God was against him. But Job persevered. Hear him: "Naked I came from my mother's womb, and naked shall I return there. The Lord gave, and the Lord has taken away; blessed be the name of the Lord. . . . Though He slay me, yet will I trust Him. Even so, I will defend my own ways before Him. . . . For I know that my Redeemer lives, and He shall stand at last on the earth. . . . He knows the way that I take; when He has tested me, I shall come forth as gold" (Job 1:21; 13:15; 19:25; 23:10). Tempted to give up or give in or give out? No wonder James said, "Look back and be challenged."

So why did James call us to "be patient" (James 5:7)? One reason is that impatience is at the root of many failures. Look back to Simon Peter: he came close to committing murder in the garden of Gethsemane (John 18:10). Look back to Moses: his impatience caused him to strike the rock instead of speaking to it as God commanded (Numbers 20:1–13). Look back to Abraham: his impatience while waiting for God's promise to be fulfilled led to the birth of Ishmael (Genesis 16:1-16). Paul affirmed the importance of patience when he wrote to the Romans: "Whatever things were written before were written for our learning, that we through the patience and comfort of the Scriptures might have hope" (Romans 15:4). "Be patient . . . until the coming of the Lord."

JUST DO IT! Here we are in the race of life. We aren't at the starting line, nor are we at the finishing tape. We're somewhere in the middle. When running a race, the start is always filled with such enthusiasm and energy. The finish holds such promise as we run the final stretch and finally reach our goal. But the middle of the race—when we're a long way from the start and not sure how far away the finish might be—is what often tests us.

Similarly, here we are—awaiting the finish, the culmination of all history, the Lord's coming again. Those who have run before us have passed the baton through the centuries, from generation to generation—without dropping it. What are we to do? Take the baton and run! And as we run, let's look up and be calm, look in and be clean, and look back and be challenged.

45   LOOK FORWARD . . . BE CONSISTENT

Above all, my brethren, do not swear, either by heaven or by earth or with any other oath. But let your "Yes" be "Yes," and your "No," "No," lest you fall into judgment.

—JAMES 5:12

*W*hile we await the blessed hope of Jesus' return, while we look forward to that glorious moment, we should live with consistency. Our lives should match what our lips say we value and believe; our walk should match our talk. Let's consider, then, the kinds of words that come out of our mouth.

When James said, "Do not swear," he was not talking about using profanity. He was saying that we should be careful about taking oaths, about saying something like "I swear I'm going to do this or that." James's point was that our word alone should be our bond. When we say yes, we should mean yes. In James's first-century world, people rarely, if ever, signed contracts as we do today. They swore oaths to each other instead. James's point was that a believer should be such a person of integrity that an oath was unnecessary.

Oaths, however, played an important part in ancient Jewish life. God even used an oath:

When God made a promise to Abraham, because He could swear by no one greater, He swore by Himself, saying, "Surely blessing I will bless you, and multiplying I will multiply you." And so, after [Abraham] had patiently endured, he obtained the promise. For men indeed swear by the greater, and an oath for confirmation is for them an end of all dispute. Thus God, determining to show more abundantly to the heirs of promise the immutability of His counsel, confirmed it by an oath. (Hebrews 6:13–17)

At one of Jesus' trials, the high priest Caiaphas provides another example of the use of an oath. We read that, as Jesus stood before Caiaphas, "Jesus kept silent. And the high priest answered and said to Him, 'I put You under oath by the living God: Tell us if You are the Christ, the Son of God!' Jesus said to him, 'It is as you said'" (Matthew 26:63–64).

Why then did James say, "Above all . . . do not swear, either by heaven or by earth or with any other oath"? By the time James wrote these words, oaths had earned a shady reputation, they were used so frequently they had lost their significance, and loopholes abounded. People were using oaths in the same way a child might say, "I cross my heart and hope to die," all the while having his fingers crossed behind his back.

Remember, too, that these instructions from James came originally from the Lord Himself. Jesus said, "Do not swear at all: neither by heaven, for it is God's throne; nor by the earth, for it is His footstool; nor by Jerusalem, for it is the city of the great King. Nor shall you swear by your head, because you cannot make one hair white or black. But let your 'Yes' be 'Yes,' and your 'No,' 'No.' For whatever is more than these is from the evil one" (Matthew 5:34–37). It's dangerous to call on God to give witness to our lies or exaggerations. He takes integrity seriously, so James was telling us to be careful to say what we mean and to mean what we say. As we look forward to the Lord's coming, we are to be sure our life is consistent with our words. What we profess on Sunday, we should practice on Monday.

Still, confusion may surround the oath we take when we have jury duty. Also, if we're a witness in a trial, we're asked to raise our right hand and say, "I swear to tell the truth, the whole truth, and nothing but the truth, so help me God." James wasn't forbidding the taking of oaths in a court of law. In our fallen and imperfect world, oaths are used in a court of law to help guard against perjury and to help ensure that truth will be spoken. Taking those oaths is a concession we believers make in the secular world. However, in church, oaths should be unnecessary. If we profess to follow Christ, we ought to truly mean what we say. We, above all others, should be men and women of integrity. As we look forward to Jesus' return, we should be consistent: our walk should match our talk.

If consistency does not characterize who we are and how we live out our faith, James warned we could be in danger of "[falling] into judgment." After all, each of us will one day give account of whether our yes was really yes and our no, really no. The fact that our Lord is coming again should motivate us to be consistent: what we say should match how we act. Remember, as we have previously noted, James's epistle is not about faith *and* works. It is not about faith *or* works. It is all about a faith *that* works, one that is characterized by words that are consistent with actions.

Finally, James was addressing believers who were living every day in anticipation of Christ's return, and so should we. These believers longed to see Jesus, touch Him, hug Him, speak to Him. We also long for Jesus' physical presence among us. We joy in His perpetual spiritual presence, but we look forward to seeing Him face-to-face.

Yet in a very real sense, this great event is not something we can get ready for. As Jesus Himself said, it will come when we least expect it, like "the lightning comes from the east and flashes to the west" (Matthew 24:27). Paul said Jesus' return would be like a "thief in the night" (1 Thessalonians 5:2). You can't *get* ready for it. You must *be* ready for it!

Jesus is coming again. And James's advice was the same to us as it was for the early church and the generations in between. Look up and be calm. Look in and be clean. Look back and be challenged. Look forward and be consistent—until the coming of the Lord.

JUST DO IT! "Let your 'Yes' be 'Yes,' and your 'No,' be 'No.'" Truth is not relative. Truth is absolute. And all truth is narrow. Mathematical truth is narrow. One plus one always equals two, never three or four. Scientific truth is narrow. Water freezes at thirty-two degrees Fahrenheit. That is very narrow. Geographical truth, historical truth, all truth is narrow. So why should we be surprised that theological truth is narrow also? Jesus said we were to enter through the "narrow gate" (Matthew 7:13).

Truth telling is always the best policy. You never have to take back what you say. You never have to worry about having all the details straight. And, you never have to be afraid of the truth. It will always triumph in the end. And truth is what will ultimately set you free (John 8:32). Let your yes be yes and your no be no. Speak truth.

46 *In* TOUCH *with a* WORLD *of* HURT

Is anyone among you suffering? Let him pray. Is anyone cheer-ful? Let him sing psalms. Is anyone among you sick? Let him call for the elders of the church, and let them pray over him, anointing him with oil in the name of the Lord. And the prayer of faith will save the sick, and the Lord will raise him up. And if he has committed sins, he will be forgiven. Confess your tres-passes to one another, and pray for one another, that you may be healed. The effective, fervent prayer of a righteous man avails much. Elijah was a man with a nature like ours, and he prayed earnestly that it would not rain; and it did not rain on the land for three years and six months. And he prayed again, and the heaven gave rain, and the earth produced its fruit.

—JAMES 5:13–18

Written twenty centuries ago, James's letter is as relevant to us in the twenty-first century as it was to those who were scattered around the Mediterranean world in the first century. We, like they, live in a world of hurt. Hearts are hurt-ing. Homes are hurting. Many individuals and families need healing. Those of us who are custodians of the gospel today should be at the forefront in recognizing and relieving those who are hurting. And James identified three primary groups of people who need hope and healing: people with pressure, people with pleasure, and people with pain.

"Is any among you suffering?" James inquired. And the response was no doubt thunderous. There is a multitude of *people dealing with pressure* all around us. Physical, emotional, or spiritual problems can rob us of joy in life. Having made his inquiry, James then offered some wise counsel. His advice was that when we are suffering, we should pray. But all too often, prayer is our last resort, not our first. Many of us attempt to do everything to relieve pressure in our lives, and when all else has failed, we sigh and say, "Well, there's nothing left to do but pray." When trouble comes knocking, our first impulse ought to be—pray.

I have seen my share of people suffering, living with intense pressure as life falls in on them. Some blame their hard times on others. Some blame God. I have seen some people go to pieces emotionally and others fall apart physically. But I have also seen believers take their burdens and lay them down at the foot of the cross. In so doing, they found peace that truly is beyond comprehension . . . His peace, the peace of Christ (Philippians 4:6–7).

God invites us to Himself, saying, "Call upon Me in the day of trouble; I will deliver you, and you shall glorify Me" (Psalm 50:15). In the New Testament, Peter reminded us that "the eyes of the Lord are on the righteous, and His ears are open to their prayers" (1 Peter 3:12). What, then, should people dealing with pressure do? Pray!

Next, James turned our attention from people with pressure to *people with pleasure*. "Is anyone cheerful?" he asked. Then "let him sing psalms" of praise. A quick clarification. Praise and thanksgiving are different. We *thank* God for what He does, and we *praise* Him for who He is, regardless of our circumstances.

If one thing should characterize our lives as Christians, it is joy. And one expression of that joy should be praise. We believers don't find our joy in what goes on outside us, but from what goes on inside us. Paul reminded us that the kingdom of God is not about any of those outside things but about "righteousness and peace and joy in the Holy Spirit" (Romans 14:17).

Prayer and praise always walk hand in hand in the Bible. The early church we read about in the book of Acts was a praying and a praising church. These believers prayed to God and praised Him when they were hurting and when they were happy. They prayed and praised Him when they lived under pressure and when they lived with pleasure. Even though they were experiencing tremendous pressure and persecution, they were a joyful people—and they are a splendid example for us.

James had yet another word of encouragement. It is offered to *people with pain*. "Is anyone among you sick?" James issued this clear directive: "Let him call for the elders of the church, and let them pray over him, anointing him with oil in the name of the Lord. And the prayer of faith will save the sick, and the Lord will raise him up." These are the only instructions in Scripture concerning how we should pray for the sick, for those in pain. And perhaps few verses in all Scripture are as misunderstood, misapplied, and misinterpreted as these.

In verses 14–15, James described ministry at a person's bedside. After all, who is more in need of healing? Is it the person who can get up, get dressed, drive to the city auditorium for a healing service, park, get out, go in, find a seat, and then stand in a line for an extended time in order to be prayed for? Or is it the person confined by pain to a hospital or hospice bed?

In these verses (we will examine them closely in the next chapter), James was not speaking about some esoteric combination of psychotherapy and an Eastern mind-over-matter technique. James was talking about believers being in touch with and involved in a hurting world. There has been a tendency in the church to gravitate toward one of two extremes when it comes to a healing ministry. Some say God's plan is that everyone be healed, that healing is but a prayer away, and that, if healing does not come, it is most likely due to sin in the sufferer's life or her lack of faith. The other extreme tends to entirely debunk any hint of the supernatural—everything these people do in the Christian religion can be explained in empirical human terminology. But God has not abdicated His throne. He is still in charge, and He can still do anything. He is very aware of and very present with people who are under pressure, in pleasure, or living with pain. And as Jesus promised on the eve of His own crucifixion, "I will not leave you orphans; I will come to you" (John 14:18).

JUST DO IT! Pray and praise—that
is good advice no matter what is happening in life. After all, God is "enthroned in the praises" of His people (Psalm 22:3). We honor Him, glorify Him, and exalt Him—our King of kings—when we praise Him. And as a dad, I learned one more thing that I'm sure God appreciates.

When our two girls were little, I would occasionally hear them say something nice about me to their friends. But what really pleased me was when they climbed up in my lap, looked in my face, and said, "Daddy, I love you."

Our heavenly Father is no different. He is pleased when we talk about Him to each other in the faith as well as when we talk about Him to those who are outside the family of faith. But what must really please Him is when you and I get alone with Him and simply praise Him for who He is and tell Him we love Him. "Is anyone among you suffering, cheerful, or sick?" Pray—and praise!

47 PEOPLE CAN HURT

Is anyone among you sick? Let him call for the elders of the church, and let them pray over him, anointing him with oil in the name of the Lord. And the prayer of faith will save the sick, and the Lord will raise him up.

—JAMES 5:14–15

*P*erhaps no other ministry of the New Testament church has been as unintentionally perverted as its healing ministry. While many of the people involved are well-intentioned and have pure hearts, others have inadvertently offered false hope to hurting people. As I said earlier, I doubt any other section of Scripture is as misinterpreted and thus misunderstood as this one.

Let's begin by establishing an important fact: our Lord is never bound by one cell He has created. He can do anything that is good—at any time—but He doesn't always heal His children who are sick. As He said in the Sermon on the Mount, God "makes His sun rise on the evil and on the good, and sends rain on the just and on the unjust" (Matthew 5:45). He is God, and He chooses whom to heal on this side of heaven and whom not to. I have realized that I don't understand much about why God heals some people and not others. It's ultimately one puzzle we must leave in the eternal councils of the Godhead.

Yet the book of James does offer some clear and concise directives as to how we are to approach the issue of healing. It is no secret that people can hurt, are hurting, and are in need of a divine touch. Let's see what God, through the pen of James, is telling us about this important subject.

THE PROBE

When James asked, "Is anyone among you sick?" he chose a precise Greek word that literally means "without strength" or "to be weak." Erroneously we often assume that James was referring only to physical sickness in these verses. This Greek word is extremely inclusive and can mean those weak in body, in soul, in mind, or in spirit. Interestingly, in the very next verse, when James said, "The prayer of faith will save the sick," he used a different word for *sick*, a word that means "to grow weary."

James was writing to those who had "grown weary" from the struggles of life, those who had been "scattered abroad" (James 1:1) in the dispersion. Having been forced to flee their jobs and homes, they were tempted to give out and give up. They were weary, and they were weak. Of course these verses can certainly apply to those with physical infirmities, but James was primarily addressing those people about to crack mentally and emotionally under the pressures of life, people who were weary and weak.

THE PROPOSAL

In such situations, James proposed, these individuals should "call for the elders of the church." The sick often need someone strong in whom they can confide, upon whom they can lean, and from whom they can draw strength. Note that the initiative falls to the person who is sick. But anyone who has ever served as a pastor has heard the complaint "No one ever called or came to visit me when I was sick." Again, in this passage, James was clear: the person who is sick is to take the initiative and call on the church to pray. When that request comes, then the elders are to perform their ministry of encouragement. As Paul exhorted, "Comfort the fainthearted [and] uphold the weak" (1 Thessalonians 5:14).

THE PROCEDURE

Then, when a sick person calls, the elders are to "pray over him, anointing him with oil in the name of the Lord." Now there are two very distinct words in Greek that we translate *anoint*. One refers to an outward anointing; literally, a "rubbing down with oil." This word is found in Jesus' story of the good Samaritan who bandaged the man's wounds, pouring oil and wine into them to fight infection and help soothe the hurt (Luke 10:34). The other New Testament word that we translate *anoint* refers to the ceremonial anointing used in a sacred and symbolic sense. Jesus, for example, once explained that the Spirit "anointed" Him to preach the gospel (Luke 4:18).

Today, anointing the sick is most often done in this ceremonial sense. A drop or two of olive oil may be placed on a finger and touched on the forehead of the sick, often in the sign of the cross. While I have personally practiced this—and there is absolutely nothing wrong with doing so—it is not at all the procedure James was describing here. James used the word that instructs us to do what the good Samaritan did. When James told us to anoint the sick with oil, he was saying that we should do all we can medicinally to help the sick person. In other words, prayer is the first resort, not the last, and we are to use the best medicine and the best doctors we can find. The church should support the efforts of the medical community to bring healing, and the medical community should support the healing efforts of the church by recognizing the power and importance of a prayer of faith.

THE PRAYER

And what is this bedside "prayer of faith"? Earlier in his letter, James indicated that when we pray, we must believe. We must "ask in faith, with no doubting, for he who doubts is like a wave of the sea driven and tossed by the wind" (James 1:6).

Furthermore, the prayer of faith must always be offered according to God's will and His Word. But until we are parents, that concept of God saying no may be harder to understand. When Susie and I were raising our daughters, we didn't always give them everything they asked for. Many times we knew what was best for them when they didn't just like our heavenly Father knows what is best for us. Quite honestly, looking back over my life, I am extremely grateful God didn't give me everything I've asked Him for! At times, my own personal preferences and prejudices clouded my thinking and definitely took precedence over His will for my life. When He did say no, I found out, time and again, that He had something better for me in mind.

In addition to submitting to God's will, the prayer of faith must be grounded in the Word of God, or it is not the prayer of faith. After all, in the words of Paul, "Faith comes by hearing, and hearing by the word of God" (Romans 10:17).

THE PROVISION

James wrote, "The prayer of faith will save the sick, and the Lord will raise him up." This verse is not, however, a guarantee that God will always heal. That "will save" statement is wrapped in the mystery of God's will and His ways. Consider that Paul once left Trophimus sick at Miletus instead of healing him (2 Timothy 4:20). Paul reported that Epaphroditus became ill and almost died (Philippians 2:25–30). Paul himself asked the Lord repeatedly to remove his own "thorn in the flesh." He realized that was not God's plan, but discovered that God's grace was sufficient (2 Corinthians 12:7, 9).

Physical healing is indeed a mystery wrapped in God's perfect will. Some people say everyone can be healed, and that is true in the sense that "with God all things are possible" (Matthew 19:26). Yet God did not heal Paul even though he asked repeatedly. Other people say illness is the direct result of sin in one's life, but some of God's greatest saints have known

some of the greatest suffering. Still others say that healing has to do with the sick person's attitude, but no one had a more pitiful attitude than Naaman, who was healed of leprosy (2 Kings 5:11–14).

Bottom line, all healing is divine. Medicine alone doesn't heal. Doctors alone don't heal. Proper diet alone doesn't heal. Exercise alone doesn't heal. *God* heals! His very name is Jehovah Rapha, "the God who heals." May we always choose to trust the One who has our best interests at heart.

JUST DO IT! People who are hurting are all around us. Maybe you who are reading these words right now are one of them. We will never understand the mysteries of why God does what He does, but we can rest in the assurance that He is a good and gracious God, our caring and wise heavenly Father. Sick? Of course get the best medical care you can and do what the doctors tell you to do. And, as James said, also call on members of your church family to pray for you. As we are about to see, "The effective, fervent prayer of a righteous man avails much" (James 5:16).

48   Perspective Can Help

Confess your trespasses to one another, and pray for one another, that you may be healed. The effective, fervent prayer of a righteous man avails much.

—JAMES 5:16

One very important factor in the equation of success or failure in life begins with the word perspective. That is, how we approach different situations, depending on an accurate (or inaccurate) perspective of what's occurring. James spoke of two important actions for believers that happen in two different directions and so require two different perspectives. One is the horizontal perspective and the command to "confess your trespasses to one another." The other is the vertical perspective and the command to "pray for one another." One action is to be directed outward in the direction of our friends, and the other, upward toward God.

THE HORIZONTAL PERSPECTIVE

When James said we should confess our sins and shortcomings to others, he was not advocating our going from one person to another filling them in on all the sordid details of moments we wish we could redo. In the dispensation of grace

in which we now live, we don't have to go through anyone or to anyone with our sin. We are privileged to be able to go straight to God, through the Lord Jesus Christ, with any and all our needs. However, at times, in order to be right with God, we need to be right with each other. In other words, to be right vertically, we must be right horizontally.

When we sin against God alone, we are to go to Him privately in prayer and ask Him to forgive us. This *private* confession is for those sins that no one needs to know about. These sins need to be confessed, but only to God.

Sometimes, however, we have sinned against another person. On these occasions we are to go to him or her personally and ask forgiveness. This is *personal* confession. Jesus said, "If you bring your gift to the altar, and there remember that your brother has something against you, leave your gift there before the altar, and go your way. First be reconciled to your brother, and then come and offer your gift" (Matthew 5:23–24). When we sin against another person, God will lay it on our hearts to make the relationship right. Personal confession can be difficult. Our general tendency is to see the wrong in the other person and often be blind to our own faults. Some of us struggle to admit even to ourselves that we have sinned against another, much less go and admit it to that person. But healing comes when we confess our trespasses to one another. Confession breaks down barriers between us and has a liberating effect on us as much as on the person we wronged.

This horizontal perspective results in horizontal action, specifically confession and restoration, and one of the most vital ministries we believers should practice is the ministry of restoration. (It is, after all, never too late for a new beginning.) As Jesus Himself said, "If your brother sins against you, go and tell him his fault between you and him alone. If he hears you, you have gained your brother" (Matthew 18:15). And the apostle Paul also called us to look horizontally: "If a man is overtaken in any trespass, you who are spiritual restore such a one in a spirit of gentleness, considering yourself lest you also be tempted" (Galatians 6:1). Keeping a horizontal perspective in life will keep us accountable to one another as we journey through this world.

THE VERTICAL PERSPECTIVE

Having called us to confess our sins to one another, James then, in the same sentence, turned our attention from the horizontal to the vertical, saying, "Pray for one another." One of the highest privileges of the Christian life is to lift our friends before the throne of grace and intercede on their behalf. It is very difficult, if not impossible, to hold something against someone if we are earnestly praying for that person daily. And with the verb tenses, James was indicating that we should make a constant practice of praying for one another.

Praying for one another means consciously seeking God's will for that person in the circumstances of his or her life. Jesus encouraged us, saying, "Ask, and it will be given to you; seek, and you will find; knock, and it will be opened to you" (Matthew 7:7). If we know His will in a matter, we are to

simply *present a petition*. We ask—and His promise is "it will be given to you."

At certain times we may not be confident about exactly what His will in a matter is. On these occasions we are to *press a petition* before Him. Jesus said, "Seek." This is a deeper level of prayer that demands an intense search for God's will. He does not want to veil His will from us, and He promises that if we keep seeking, we "will find."

Then at other times we are quite sure of God's overall will in a matter, but for some reason we do not see the details that will lead us to a specific answer. What are we to do in such times? We are to *persist in our petition*. We are to knock, and the verb tense indicates we are not to quit; instead, we are to keep on knocking. And, again, we have His promise: "It will be opened to you."

Perspective is vital in Christian living. And to live a strong and healthy Christian life, we need to be tuned in to relationships on the horizontal plane as well as the vertical.

JUST DO IT! "Confess your trespasses to one another, and pray for one another." Sometimes our sins are private in nature. At other times our sins are personal: we have hurt or offended someone else. And sometimes a person is guilty of public sin that damages the entire body of Christ. If your sin is private, keep it that way. There is no need to confess it to anyone else. Simply go to God in repentance and confession, for "if we confess our sins, He is faithful and just to forgive us" (1 John 1:9). If your sin is personal, then confess it not only to God, but also to the person you offended. But you're not done yet: seek reconciliation. If your sin is public in nature, at times you may need an honest confession and a public apology from a truly repentant heart.

Here is the good news: "The blood of Jesus Christ [God's] Son cleanses us from *all* sin" (1 John 1:7, emphasis added). Remember, it's never too late for a new beginning!

49   PRAYERS CAN HEAL

The effective, fervent prayer of a righteous man avails much. Elijah was a man with a nature like ours, and he prayed earnestly that it would not rain; and it did not rain on the land for three years and six months. And he prayed again, and the heaven gave rain, and the earth produced its fruit.

—JAMES 5:16–18

*I*f there is one thing to be said about the Greek language, it is that it's one of the most expressive languages in all the earth. Consider, for example, that in English we have only one word for love. Whether we are saying, "I love my wife" or "I love golf" or "I love my dog" or "I love chocolate" or even "I love the Lord," we use the same word for love. The Greeks, however, have several words for love: one to express the highest level of love—the kind that truly reflects God's love, another to express fondness or affection for someone, and still another to refer to physical attraction.

Likewise, Greek has several words that we translate as "prayer" in English. The word for prayer in James 5:16 carries with it the idea of humbly begging for something, making an earnest plea. This isn't a prayer that orders God to do this or that, nor is it one that claims a certain thing. This word suggests a needy man with his head bowed and his cap rolled up in his hands, humbly asking for help, not demanding it or claiming something he feels is due him. This humble prayer is approached with integrity, asked with intensity, and answered with immensity.

A PRAYER THAT IS APPROACHED WITH INTEGRITY

James said that an effective prayer is the prayer of "a righteous man." This requirement may seem a bit threatening. Our first response may be "That leaves me out!" The word *righteous* has a rather foreboding ring to it. Knowing this, James inserted an illustration of the fact that "the effective, fervent prayer of a righteous man avails much." He mentioned Elijah and said that this great man of God was "a man with a nature like ours." One minute he could be on the mountaintop celebrating and the next minute, under the juniper tree sulking. Elijah could be attacking huge problems head-on one minute and running from them the next. He was ordinary. He was just like you and just like me—and he was righteous. Simply put, Elijah was right with God. James wasn't parading out super saints here. Just folks like you and me. For all believers are "righteous" as we stand before God clothed in the righteousness of Christ. Paul said, "[God] made [Jesus] who knew no sin to be sin for us, that we might become the righteousness of God in Him" (2 Corinthians 5:21). In Christ, we are clothed in His righteousness.

But if spiritual righteousness is the only issue here, why

aren't more of our prayers answered? When James said the prayer of "a righteous man" avails much, he had in mind moral righteousness. He was speaking of the kind of integrity that John addressed in his epistle: "He who practices righteousness is righteous, just as He is righteous" (1 John 3:7). The emphasis is on *doing* righteousness, not merely *being* righteous in God's eyes. Righteous people practice what they preach. They are men and women of integrity. John added, "Whatever we ask we receive from Him, because we keep His commandments and *do* those things that are pleasing in His sight" (1 John 3:22, emphasis added). Prayer can heal a world of hurt when we approach the Lord with integrity.

A PRAYER THAT IS ASKED WITH INTENSITY

James was not talking about just any prayer, but about prayer that is "fervent." We derive our English word *energy* from this Greek wording. Literally, it means "to be stretched out," and it suggests an athlete stretching out toward the finish line with a final burst of energy. When we are striving to run the Christian race in obedience to Christ, our prayers take on a powerful and persuasive energy. They become fervent.

Prayers that get results are not long, drawn-out orations. They are pointed and powerful, asked with intensity and approached with integrity. They are prayers like that of the publican, "God, be merciful to me a sinner" (Luke 18:13). These fervent prayers are like the one Simon Peter prayed while sinking in the sea, "Lord, save me!" (Matthew 14:30).

They are prayers like Jacob's, "I will not let you go unless you bless me!" (Genesis 32:26).

It is not the length of your prayers but the depth of your prayers that makes them effective. It is not the prayers that issue forth from your head, but the prayers that spring from your heart that are effective. So approach God with integrity, do those things He commands, and then pray with passion and intensity. Why? Because "the effective, fervent prayer of a righteous man avails much."

A PRAYER THAT IS ANSWERED WITH IMMENSITY

This prayer James described "avails much." When we are doing what is right—when we are praying in humility with a spirit of energetic fervor—God answers our prayers. Elijah, "a man with a nature like ours," knew that truth. He approached God with integrity; he was a doer of the word, not just a hearer (James 1:22); and he asked with intensity. No wonder God answered with immensity and sent the rain to soak the parched land.

Before we finish looking at James 5:16, remember that we are in the section of James's letter that deals with healing. One might find it a bit strange that James would use Elijah as an illustration here. Why not Naaman who was healed of leprosy? Why not the Shunammite woman's son who was brought back to life? Why Elijah? Because primarily James was addressing our spiritual and emotional well-being, not just our physical well-being. Elijah's prayers opened up heaven, and the

Almighty sent refreshing rain upon a drought-stricken earth. And isn't rain from heaven the real need of hearts that are hungry and souls that are dry?

God is still in the business of divinely intervening in the natural processes He established so long ago. Sometimes He uses doctors and medicine, but God Himself is the ultimate healer. James said, "The Lord will raise him up" (James 5:15). We will pray bolder prayers when we remember that God can do anything. When we pray, we are talking to a God who isn't limited by time or space or anything He has ever created. He is, therefore, a God who answers our prayers with immensity. Effective prayer can make a difference in a world filled with hurting people.

God, help us to reach up to You with "effective, fervent" prayers, and then to be Your hands extended in reaching out to people in need.

JUST DO IT! Let me close this chapter with an awesome truth: God answers prayer. Don't rush past that last sentence. Read it again: God really does answer prayer! If more of us truly believed this, we would spend more time talking *to* Him than just talking *about* Him. God always answers our prayers, and, sometimes His answer is *direct.* We pray and we immediately see the answer. Other times, His answer is *delayed.* For His own good reason, He places us in a holding pattern. Still other times, God's answer is *different*. He does answer but differently than we expected, yet always for our own good. And then at times our request is *denied*. God simply says, "No." And one reason He says no is because He always knows what is best for us.

50   It's Never Too Late *for a* New Beginning

Brethren, if anyone among you wanders from the truth, and someone turns him back, let him know that he who turns a sinner from the error of his way will save a soul from death and cover a multitude of sins.

—JAMES 5:19–20

*F*or years a beautiful antique table has graced the entryway of our home. But when I first saw it, there was nothing of beauty about it. Only the promise of beauty.

We acquired the table more than forty years ago during the days of our first pastorate out on the plains of southwestern Oklahoma. The little farming community of Hobart was undergoing a transition. The kids of those wheat farmers went away to college but never came back to the farms. Instead, after earning their degrees, they made their way to the big cities, the site of expanding employment opportunities. So when the parents died, no one would take over the family farms, and their household possessions were often sold at auctions. Those Saturday auctions were the place to be, and crowds of people came from all the nearby farms and towns.

That antique table caught my eye at one of those farm-house auctions. For many years, probably decades, it had just sat out in the barn. Chickens had roosted on it. Old greasy tools had sat on it. In fact, through the years all sorts of trash had been thrown on it. It was filthy and flimsy, and when the auctioneer called its number, no one even made a bid on it. So I did. I bought that old table for just a couple of dollars and the next week took it to a man in Hobart who loved to restore old furniture items in a shed behind his house. He stripped it down to its bare wood and, over the course of several days, restored it to the thing of beauty it once was. To this day that table is one of our most cherished possessions and conversation pieces.

Like my friend in Hobart, God Himself is in the restoration business. As I've said before in these pages, it is never too late for a new beginning for anyone. And what is even more remarkable, He uses folks like you and me to help people find a new beginning. There are people all around us who have been relegated to an old barn somewhere, beaten and broken by life's circumstances, and finally put off to the side where they began to lose their beauty. But there is a land of beginning again—for any and all of us.

In addition to needing the opportunity to begin again, all of us need a partner in ministry. James certainly had a great one in Peter. They, in effect, served as co-pastors of the church in Jerusalem, and together they convened the great Jerusalem Council (Acts 15). These two men were the undisputed leaders of the early church.

It may well be that James had Peter in mind when he penned these words because if ever someone needed restoration and a new beginning, it was Simon Peter. You probably remember the story well. Peter had been so self-confident and boastful about his commitment to the Lord Jesus, boldly asserting that even if all the others turned back, he would always stay true to his Lord. And Peter was true to his word until the heat was turned up! Jesus had been arrested and subsequently been interrogated by Caiaphas, the Jews' chief priest. Peter "followed at a distance" (Luke 22:54), and when he was recognized as one of the Galilean followers of Christ, Peter denied it three times. As Jesus had prophesied, the rooster then crowed to signal the coming dawn. But Peter, remembering Jesus' earlier warning that he would betray Him, went out and "wept bitterly" (v. 62). Later, however, the resurrected Christ met Peter and some of the disciples on the north shore of the Sea of Galilee. There Jesus provided Peter with three opportunities to reaffirm his love for Him. Peter's second chance was not only possible, but it was also profitable. Simon Peter never turned back. Restored, he became the rock who led the church into its greatest days of expansion (Matthew 16:18).

The Bible contains many accounts of men and women who got a second chance and, by God's grace, used it well. Who would have picked a murderer to deliver a nation from slavery and lead them to freedom? God did. Moses had blown it (Exodus 2:11–14). But forty years in obscurity on the backside of a desert enabled him to take advantage of the second chance God gave him, and he became the great emancipator of his people. And what about the lustful fellow who was described as a "man after God's own heart" (2 Samuel 11:1–27; 1 Samuel 13:14)? Read David's prayer of repentance in Psalm 51 and see what qualifies people for a second chance. And what about Jonah? He got his do-over: "The word of the Lord came to Jonah the second time" (Jonah 3:1). He also found that a second chance is possible for anyone.

The second chance is possible, but it is not automatic. Judas didn't get a second chance. Why? He didn't repent, so he didn't receive the opportunity to be restored. Do you remember the rich young ruler? He didn't get a second chance either. He was remorseful upon hearing the demands of discipleship and "went away sorrowful." Sorrow is not the same as repentance. This rich young man didn't repent so he was not restored. And what about Pontius Pilate, the Roman governor who condemned Jesus to death? He washed his hands in a basin of water, regretting that he had done as the crowd demanded, but Pilate did not repent. The second chance is possible but not automatic. It is reserved for people like Simon Peter, who don't merely feel remorse or try to reform, but who truly repent. That is, they change their minds, which results in a change of action; and as they do so, they find a new beginning.

Simon Peter definitely took advantage of his second chance. He went from his seaside meeting with Christ to become the powerful preacher of Pentecost, and his message brought about the birth of the church. We find Peter over and over in

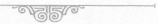

the book of Acts being imprisoned and beaten yet saying, "We cannot but speak the things which we have seen and heard" (Acts 4:20). Tradition tells us he met a martyr's death by crucifixion. But telling his executioners that he was unworthy to die in the same manner as his Savior, he requested to be crucified upside down. And so he was.

James closed his letter with the important reminder that sin can wreck hearts, homes, plans, and people. But your sin can never keep God from loving you. James was shouting again now. Can you hear him? "It is never too late for a new beginning!"

Every time I walk past that antique table, I am reminded that God specializes in the restoration business. All of us know people who are like that old table used to be, who are battered and bruised and have been stuck in the back corners of life, having lost their beauty, and who are not being used for any real purpose. James concluded his letter with this challenge to us: take the sinners and the broken people we know by the hand and bring them to the One who can make old things pass away and make all things become new.

JUST DO IT! God desires that all of us get into the restoration business. Paul framed it like this: "If a man is overtaken in any trespass, you who are spiritual restore such a one in a spirit of gentleness, considering yourself lest you also be tempted.

Bear one another's burdens, and so fulfill the law of Christ" (Galatians 6:1–2). In the Greek, the word *restore* is from a medical term that means "to set a broken bone." When someone breaks a bone in his or her arm, a doctor sets it, realigning it and then putting a cast on it to keep it in place as it heals. Then during about six weeks, God does the actual healing.

Our job is to find those broken people who need a second chance. We are to restore them: we are to help get their lives and priorities lined up with Scripture and God's will. Once that realigning is done, God can then do the healing. After all, it's never too late for a new beginning.

51 *The* POSSIBILITY *of* OUR FALLING

Brethren, if anyone among you wanders from the truth, and someone turns him back, let him know that he who turns a sinner from the error of his way will save a soul from death and cover a multitude of sins.

—JAMES 5:19–20

With this word of warning, James closed his letter. Notice, though, how his warning aligns with Paul's warning to us: "Let him who thinks he stands take heed lest he fall" (1 Corinthians 10:12). All of us live with the possibility that we, too, might easily wander from the truth. Let's learn from James, then, about the person, the path, and the place of our potential wandering.

THE PERSON HERE IS A DISCIPLE

James was addressing one "among you," a group he called his "brethren," people who were his brothers and sisters in the faith. The word *brethren* means "one who shares with another a mutual life."

Susie and I have two daughters, Wendy and Holly. We are

their natural parents. They share our life. Our blood courses through their veins. Likewise, when we are born into God's family, we share in His life. As Peter said, we have become "partakers of the divine nature" (2 Peter 1:4). We are God's children, and thus we share with our brothers and sisters in faith—the life of Christ. We have a special relationship with one another. In a very real sense, we are more closely related to one another through the blood of Christ than to our own blood relatives who do not know Him.

So here James was talking to a group of believers about another believer—a brother or sister—"anyone among you." This verse doesn't apply to the person without Christ. James knew that it is possible for a true believer to wander from the truth, but that wandering doesn't mean that such a fallen one is no longer a Christian. A person truly born into God's family through the new birth (John 3) can never sever that relationship. James likened spiritual birth to physical birth: it only takes place once. When your physical child disobeys you, that behavior doesn't sever the relationship. That behavior doesn't mean he or she is no longer your child. That son or daughter has been born into your family, and although your fellowship might be damaged, your relationship can never be severed. James was saying that one's fellowship with God might be damaged. But the good news is it can be restored.

James introduced this statement about the possibility of our falling with the word *if*. This is a warning for the future. *If* is like a flashing yellow warning light designed to get our attention as we approach various intersections of life: "if anyone among you wanders from the truth." Life has many intersections. James was telling us to make sure that we see the caution light, we look both ways, and we do not make a wrong turn. The person he was talking about here could be any one of us believers.

THE PATH HERE IS DECEPTIVE

James said it is possible for us to "wander from the truth." *To wander* means "to go astray." It is a gradual moving away from the will and way of God. Jesus used the same Greek word when He told the story of the shepherd who had a hundred sheep, one of which "goes astray" (Matthew 18:12). How did that sheep go astray? It didn't intend to do so. It just wandered from a little patch of grass here to a little patch of grass there, keeping its head down all the way, just guided by its appetite. Before the little sheep realized what happened, it had wandered away from the security and safety of its shepherd.

And that is the way we believers go astray as well. We never set out intending to wander from the Lord, His will, and His ways. Our straying happens gradually. Peter used this same word, saying, "You were like sheep going astray." Then, acknowledging the possibility of our falling, Peter continued with the truth that it is never too late for a new beginning: "But [you who strayed] have now returned to the Shepherd and Overseer of your souls" (1 Peter 2:25).

Wandering away from God can happen so subtly.

THE PLACE HERE IS DOCTRINAL

Note that James was saying that our wandering is "from the truth." Jesus affirmed that He Himself was the embodiment of truth when, on the night before His crucifixion, He said, "I am the way, the truth, and the life. No one comes to the Father except through Me" (John 14:6). And, in His high intercessory prayer to the Father, Jesus prayed to God, "Sanctify [these disciples] by Your truth. Your word is truth" (John 17:17). James was warning us not to stray from the truth of God's Word. We must never put our convictions on the shelf. If we don't make a deliberate effort to stay close to the truth, we will wander from it. After all, we live in a world with lots of distractions.

And in this world many people are on a quest for unity at all costs and are therefore devaluing the importance of doctrinal truth in the Christian life. However, doctrine matters—and it matters greatly. If a culture believes that human beings are nothing more than descendants of monkeys, it will not be long before raw animalistic tendencies begin to dominate our lifestyles, greatly threatening a civilized society. On the other hand, if we believe that we are God's special creations, knit together by Him, "fearfully and wonderfully made" and given an eternal purpose in life, we will begin to act like the human beings made in His very image that we are (Psalm 139:13–14, 16). If we believe we are not some random act of science but instead possess a spirit that can connect with God, that belief will affect our behavior. Never fall victim to the lie that doctrinal truth is not important. What we truly believe ultimately determines how we behave.

It is possible for any of us to wander away from the place of sound doctrine and truth. When we wander from doctrine, we will wander from duty. When we wander from belief, our wandering behavior is sure to follow. Yes, it is absolutely possible for any one of us to wander from a place of solid doctrine and God's eternal truth. But the second chance is possible as well. It is never too late for any of us to find a new beginning.

JUST DO IT! You are not simply the result of some random act of nature. No one has a thumbprint like yours. No one on the planet has— no one in history has ever had—DNA exactly like yours. Think about that. You are a unique individual, indescribably special to God. There is no one like you. And there is something for you to do in life that no one can do quite like you can. There is a purpose in your life. You have a mission. Look at the flashing yellow light at this intersection in your life. Don't wander from the truth. It is the only thing that will ultimately set you free (John 8:32). What you believe is determining how you behave. Believe in Jesus and follow Him—for He is *the* Truth!

52   *The* RESPONSIBILITY *of* OUR CALLING

Brethren, if anyone among you wanders from the truth, and someone turns him back, let him know that he who turns a sinner from the error of his way will save a soul from death and cover a multitude of sins.

—JAMES 5:19–20

*O*ur calling in the Christian life comes with a responsibility not only to Christ but also to one another in the family of faith. We have the responsibility of helping to bring back any fellow believers who have wandered from God's truth. Paul referred to this as "the ministry of reconciliation" that we have toward one another (2 Corinthians 5:18). He also admonished us, saying, "Brethren, if a man is overtaken in any trespass, you who are spiritual restore such a one in a spirit of gentleness, considering yourself lest you also be tempted" (Galatians 6:1). In James's words we are to "[turn] him back." Again, this is the responsibility of our calling, the responsibility we have to Christ and to one another.

For too many believers, though, the first reaction to learning that someone has fallen is to rush to the phone, make a

quick call, and ask, "Did you hear about . . . ?" Sadly, we may be better known for our pointed fingers of accusation and insinuation than for our broken hearts and earnest desire to help those who wander from the truth.

In our zeal to win the lost for Christ, we sometimes forget we also have a responsibility to, in a sense, win the saved. We are responsible for trying to turn "a sinner from the error of his way [and thereby] save a soul from death and cover a multitude of sins."

A CALL TO REPENTANCE

It's good to know we can come back to the Lord and start over again. One failure does not make us a flop. We can recognize our mistakes, return to the intersection where we made the wrong turn, and take the better path.

When James spoke of turning back someone "from the error of his way," he was speaking of repentance. The same word is found in Jesus' conversation with Simon Peter: "I have prayed for you, that your faith should not fail; and when you have [turned back] to Me, strengthen your brethren" (Luke 22:32).

James was not referring to people here who are sorry only because they were caught in a particular sin. He was talking to those sinners who have strayed and who truly come back, who turn from "the error of [their] way." Repentance is the key that opens the door of restoration with God.

The Lord Jesus told the greatest story ever to illustrate true repentance. You may know it well. It is the story of a young man who wandered from the truth. The bright lights of the big city held a fascination for him, so he took his inheritance and left home. He thought he would find a good time, but all he found were hangovers, rip-offs, and unemployment lines when he ran out of money. Ending up in a pigpen feeding swine (not an ideal job for a nice Jewish boy), he decided to get up and go home. His turning back—his repentance—involved three steps. First, he changed his *mind*. The Bible says, "He came to himself" (Luke 15:17). This change of mind brought about a change of his *will*, his volition. He said, "I *will* arise and go to my father" (v. 18, emphasis added). Then his *actions* changed: "He arose and came to his father" (v. 20).

Repentance is a change of mind that brings about a change of the will and results in a change of action, a turning back. When we, like this boy, see the error of our ways and turn back to God's path for our life, we will find our heavenly Father responding the same way he found his father: no pointed fingers of accusation, no arms crossed in disgust, and no clenched fists. Just open arms, wide, loving, and forgiving open arms.

A CALL TO RESUSCITATION

Returning to James's statement, he said whoever "turns a sinner from the error of his way will save a soul from death." James was referring here to physical death, not eternal death, not eternal separation from God. The Bible calls it "the sin leading to death." The apostle John described it this way: "If anyone sees his brother sinning a sin which does not lead to death, he will ask, and He will give him life for those who commit sin not leading to death. There is sin leading to death" (1 John 5:16). At times when a believer becomes rebellious and refuses to repent, God will take him or her out prematurely through physical death. That's why, when we can bring our brothers and sisters back to Jesus, we just might be saving them from death.

Remember Ananias and his wife, Sapphira? Their story, recorded in Acts 5, is a classic example of this "sin unto death." The church was in its infancy, and this couple lied to the apostles and—worse—to the Holy Spirit. God struck them dead on the spot. He didn't take their lives in order to get even with them. In His mercy, God dismissed this couple from earth in order to keep them from further sin and to protect the witness of His infant church.

Because Moses sinned in the wilderness when he struck the rock instead of just speaking to it, he was not allowed to enter the promised land. Moses died on Mt. Nebo after viewing the long-promised land from a distance. The Bible clearly says there is a sin unto death.

When Christians fall out of the will of God and refuse to repent, God often chastens them, sometimes even with death. This course of action is not for us to judge, but we can trust that God knows the motives of a person's heart: "The Lord does not see as man sees; for man looks at the outward appearance, but the Lord looks at the heart" (1 Samuel 16:7).

A CALL TO RESTORATION

James was clear: when we are involved in this ministry of reconciliation and restoration, we "cover a multitude of sins" in the process. The person who repents and returns to the Lord has the promise of having his or her sins covered. This is made possible for us at an extraordinarily high cost: the blood of Jesus shed on Calvary's cross for our sins. King David expressed our heartfelt feelings at this point: "Blessed is he whose transgression is forgiven, whose sin is covered" (Psalm 32:1).

When a Christian repents of his sin and turns back to God, he finds complete restoration, and his transgressions are removed "as far as the east is from the west" (Psalm 103:12). God cannot and will not see our sins after we have been cleansed by the blood of Jesus Christ. In David's powerful, penitent prayer, we read that it was not his salvation he longed to have restored, but his joy. "Restore to me the joy of Your salvation" was his passionate desire and plea to God (Psalm 51:12).

It is a wonderful privilege to know that God calls upon us and allows us to be His agents in helping others in the restoration process. Look again at the promise that closes James's book: "If anyone among you wanders from the truth, and someone turns him back, let him know that he who turns a sinner from the error of his way will save a soul from death and cover a multitude of sins."

And with this statement James abruptly ended his letter.

James's closing stands in stark contrast to the encouraging and loving way that Paul, Peter, and Jude, for example, ended their New Testament epistles. I think that James's ending is rather abrupt because he was a practical man. Having told us what we ought to do, James said in effect, "Now get on with it! Just do it!"

JUST DO IT! We now close our study of the book of James, but not before a final reminder of a twofold principle in place throughout its chapters and verses. First, *every sin we try to cover up, God will uncover.* Aware of that fact, Paul reminded us to "judge nothing before the time, until the Lord comes, who will both bring to light the hidden things of darkness and reveal the counsels of the hearts" (1 Corinthians 4:5). But the good news is this: *every sin we uncover, God will cover.* Consider this Old Testament promise: "He who covers his sins will not prosper, but whoever confesses and forsakes them will have mercy" (Proverbs 28:13). Go ahead! Confess and forsake your sin, and God will cover it with the blood of Christ. There is no good reason to wait! Just do it!

EPILOGUE

*T*hroughout Christian history the thrust of James's message to those first-century "scattered" believers—and to us as well—has been misunderstood. So, here at the end of the book, let me state it one more time. James's message is not about faith *and* works. It is not about faith *or* works. It is about a faith *that* works.

Faith always precedes any lasting good work. So we begin applying James's message to our lives not by *trying* harder, but by *trusting* our entire being to Christ and His finished redemptive work on our behalf. The Christian life is not a *changed* life. It is not that we, all of a sudden, take on a new set of moral standards and try hard to change our ways. Instead, the Christian life is an *exchanged* life. We confess our sin and give God our old life. In response He forgives our sin and gives us a brand-new life: Christ comes to live in us, never to leave us, and empowers us to serve Him and His people. Once we are filled with God's Holy Spirit, we can begin the great adventure of finding our true purpose for which He created us in the first place.

In fact, this new life is God's free gift to us. The Bible says, "The wages of sin is death, but the gift of God is eternal life in Christ Jesus our Lord" (Romans 6:23). We cannot earn our

salvation, and we do not deserve it. God gives us our transformed and eternal life because of His love and His grace, and we receive that gift through faith alone, by putting our faith in Him. We are all sinners who fall far short of God's holy standards for our lives.

Yet God is a God of love who loves us despite our sin, and at the same time He is a God of justice who must punish sin. And this is where Jesus steps in. He is the holy and sinless God-man who came into this sin-filled world to take your sin onto His own body and, on your behalf, suffer God's judgment of your sin on the cross. But just knowing this gospel truth is not enough. You must transfer your trust for this life from yourself and your own human efforts to Christ alone, and you must place your faith in Jesus, believing that His death and resurrection achieved for you God's forgiveness and your personal salvation.

Jesus said, "Behold, I stand at the door and knock. If anyone hears My voice and opens the door, I will come in to him" (Revelation 3:20). So picture an imaginary door on your heart and know that Jesus is knocking on it right now. If you would like to receive this gift of eternal and abundant life, you can respond to Jesus now, at this very moment. He promises that "whoever calls on the name of the LORD shall be saved" (Romans 10:13).

If you're not quite sure how to respond, here is a prayer you can pray. Go ahead—in your heart—pray it:

Dear Lord Jesus, I know I have sinned. I know I don't deserve eternal life. Please forgive me for my sin. Thank You for taking my sin onto Your body and dying on the cross in my place. I trust that You are the only One who can save me from eternal separation from a holy God. So I ask You to be Lord and King in my life. I turn my face to You, accepting Your gracious offer of forgiveness and eternal life. Thank You, Lord, for coming into my life as my Savior and my Lord. In Jesus' name I pray. Amen.

A simple prayer cannot save you, but Jesus can . . . and He will. If you did pray this prayer—and if this prayer reflects the desire of your heart—you can claim the promise Jesus made to those who would follow Him: "Most assuredly . . . he who believes in Me has everlasting life" (John 6:47).

You are now ready for the great adventure and purpose for which you were created: you can know Christ and walk through life with Him. As you do, His Spirit will work in you to transform you, to make you more like Him in character.

One more thought. Being comes before doing because what we *do* is always determined by what we *are* or whose we *are*. You *are* a child of God. So begin now to *do* all that James has instructed God's people to do. After all, our Christian faith is a faith *that* works. So just do it!

MISSION:DIGNITY

*A*ll of the author's royalties and any proceeds from *The James Code*, *The Jesus Code*, and *The Joshua Code* go to the support of Mission:Dignity, a ministry of the Dallas-based GuideStone Financial Resources that enables thousands of retired ministers (and, in most cases, their widows) who are living near the poverty level, to live out their days with dignity and security. Many of them spent their pastoral ministry in small churches that were unable to provide adequately for their retirement. They also lived in church-owned parsonages and, upon their vocational retirement, had to vacate them as well. Mission:Dignity is a way of letting these good and godly servants know they are not forgotten and will be cared for in their declining years.

All of the expenses of this ministry are paid out of an endowment that has been raised for such, so that everyone who gives to Mission:Dignity can be assured that every cent of their gift goes to one of these precious saints in need.

For additional information regarding this ministry, please go to *www.guidestone.org* and click on the Mission:Dignity icon, or call toll-free at 1-888-98-GUIDE (1-888-984-8433).

TRANSFORM THE HEARTS OF YOUR CONGREGATION WITH

God's Word

The Joshua Code is designed to walk you through a year-long journey of meditating on one verse a week in order to recall and recite Scripture at will. Topics include temptation, understanding salvation, prayer, grace, vision, integrity, and more.

The Jesus Code takes you on a journey with one critical question each week to study and meditate on until the answer is firmly fixed in your mind and heart. Those answers will show God's will for your life, and they will help you feel confident as you share your faith with others.

100% of the author's royalties and proceeds goes to support Mission:Dignity—a ministry providing support for impoverished retired pastors and missionaries.

ABOUT *the* AUTHOR

$\mathcal{F}$or more than twenty-five years, O. S. Hawkins served pastorates including the First Baptist Church in Fort Lauderdale, Florida, and the First Baptist Church in Dallas, Texas. A native of Fort Worth, he has three earned degrees (BBA, MDiv, and DMin) as well as several honorary degrees. He is president of GuideStone Financial Resources, which serves 250,000 pastors, church staff members, missionaries, doctors, nurses, university professors, and other workers in various Christian organizations with their retirement and benefit service needs. He is the author of more than twenty-five books, including the bestselling *The Joshua Code* and *The Jesus Code*, and preaches regularly at conferences, universities, business groups, and churches across the nation. He and his wife, Susie, have two married daughters and six grandchildren.

 Follow O. S. Hawkins on Twitter @oshawkins

Visit www.oshawkins.com for hundreds of free
leadership and personal growth resources.